Advertising Financial Products and Services

Recent Titles from
Quorum Books

Advertising Financial Products and Services

PROVEN TECHNIQUES AND PRINCIPLES FOR BANKS, INVESTMENT FIRMS, INSURANCE COMPANIES, AND THEIR AGENCIES

Alec Benn

QUORUM BOOKS

NEW YORK • WESTPORT, CONNECTICUT • LONDON

Library of Congress Cataloging-in-Publication Data

Benn, Alec.
  Advertising financial products and services.

  Includes index.
  1. Bank Marketing.   2. Financial institutions—
Marketing.   3. Insurance companies—Marketing.
I. Title.
HG1616.M3B43   1986   659.1'93321   85–24406
ISBN 0–89930–103–7 (lib. bdg. : alk. paper)

Library of Congress Catalog Card Number: 85–24406
ISBN: 0–89930–103–7

First published in 1986 by Quorum Books

Greenwood Press, Inc.
88 Post Road West, Westport, Connecticut 06881

Printed in the United States of America

The paper used in this book complies with the
Permanent Paper Standard issued by the National
Information Standards Organization (Z39.48–1984).

10 9 8 7 6 5 4 3 2 1

To Caroline M. Benn

CONTENTS

CASE HISTORIES

INVESTING

INSURANCE

CASE HISTORIES BY
FINANCIAL ORGANIZATION

OTHER ILLUSTRATIONS

OTHER FEATURES

ACKNOWLEDGMENTS

I especially thank Stephen S. Fenichell and Caroline M. Benn for reading the entire manuscript and making valuable suggestions, and Philip C. Sievers for his valuable comments on part of the manuscript.

I also thank Richard Fernandes, J. Luttrell Maclin, William L. Clayton, Claude P. Fromm, Ken Vernon, Arthur Kennedy, Jeff Williamson, Robert H. Nutt, Edward J. Pfeiffer, Eve Slakter, Irwin Menchel, Michael Knaisch, Andrew P. Mayo, Betsy Clark, and Gordon M. Gumpertz. I appreciate their help and that of others, particularly those who suggested case histories that were not used for one reason or another, often because of duplication.

Advertising Financial Products and Services

PART I
WHAT TO DO

1

HOW FINANCIAL ADVERTISING DIFFERS AND WHY IT IS MORE DIFFICULT THAN OTHER KINDS OF ADVERTISING

The head of a large general advertising agency widely admired for its apparent creativity was continually criticizing financial advertising as "unimaginative"—until the agency obtained an investment banking account.

The agency required nearly a year to produce a usable advertisement—and then the full-page ad in *The Wall Street Journal* and *The New York Times* featured a huge telephone, meant to symbolize the importance of making a telephone call to the advertiser. The illustration took up over three-quarters of the page.

Since the advertisement was for a major investment banking firm that did not deal with individual investors, the target audience was presumably corporate officers who could choose or influence the choice of an underwriter. Not only would most of this audience ignore the ad, believing it to be for telephone equipment—for which many ads were appearing at the time—but even those readers who guessed it was an investment ad from the big signature probably presumed it was about the breakup of AT&T, which was occurring at the time.

The agency had tripped on one of the many hurdles peculiar to all financial advertising—banking and insurance advertising as well as investment advertising. Finance is abstract. Seldom can a product be pictured. Deposits, loans, securities, annuities, advice, and credit are all intangible. But most advertising people are accustomed to centering the appeal of the ads they create or guide on the physical appearance of a tangible product. Coffee commercials show coffee being pleasantly consumed and close-ups of the beans and the can. Paper towel commercials show a towel being used to wipe up a liquid. With few exceptions, automobile ads feature the looks of the car. Even in those famous original Volkswagen ads, a photograph of the Beetle took up most of the space. In fashion, travel, and cosmetics advertisements, picturing the product is fundamental.

Picturing the product succeeds because it attracts readers of newspapers and magazines and holds the attention of television viewers who are prospective buyers. A person interested in buying an automobile has an avid interest in pictures of automobiles. Further, in package goods advertising, picturing the can or box is not only desirable but essential, so shoppers will know what to look for in the supermarket.

But picturing a product that has little connection with what is being advertised attracts people interested in the pictured product, not those who might be buyers of what is being advertised—except by coincidence. The telephone in the investment banking ad attracted the attention of people interested in telephones. Instead of acting as a magnet to increase the number of true prospects, the telephone illustration acted as a screen—especially because the headline was so small that it couldn't attract many readers on its own. The readership was reduced to people who were interested in telephones and to competitors, who, noting the logo, wondered what the advertiser was up to.

In featuring a telephone, the agency was apparently trying to avoid creating an advertisement that would look similar to other financial ads. Because of the abstract nature of finance, most financial advertisements are all type, or feature people or animals, or include a small illustration of a booklet. Financial TV commercials feature people and animals even more often, although one major investment firm's television commercials in the early 1980s were all type. The abstract nature of financial advertising makes it difficult to do anything else without damaging the effectiveness of the advertisement (yet dramatic illustrations are often possible, as several case histories in this book show).

Writing about finance is also difficult because of its abstract nature. Proponents of clear and interesting writing continually exhort students to "Be concrete" but it is difficult to be concrete when describing return on a money market account, earnings per share, or the actuarial intricacies of insurance.

The difficulty of making abstract concepts concrete, and thus emotionally stimulating, is compounded by the fact that the key benefit in financial advertising—a low interest rate on loans, a high return on an investment, a low premium on insurance—can usually best be communicated as a percentage. But many prospects for financial services can't recognize the significance of a percentage. Most elementary school students dislike arithmetic, and that dislike can stick with them throughout life. Most readers, viewers, and listeners don't have the necessary aptitude to easily figure out, much less get an emotional charge out of, the relationship between percentages. A financial expert can readily see that 12% is 20% more than 10%—and get enthusiastic about even slighter differentials—but such a congregation of numbers would simply confuse the average prospect for a financial service.

Further, most prospects don't have the background to know the significance of a number standing alone. Most don't know exactly what return they are currently getting on their money market accounts, or the precise yields on their stocks, for example. Thus, even if they could easily relate one percentage to another, they would be vague about the comparison.

So the best financial advertising translates a *percentage* benefit into an easy-to-understand, directly emotional *word* benefit—but the ad includes the actual percentages for the arithmetic-minded and for accurate substantiation.

Successful financial advertising actually requires as much or more imagination than other types of advertising, but in financial advertising the imagination used is rarely obvious.

Many copywriters have difficulty turning a percentage benefit into an emotional, word benefit because they don't have a feeling for numbers. They're word-minded, like most people. Further, the conversion may not be fully appreciated by the advertiser. Many of the exceptional students who liked arithmetic end up in finance. Like many advertisers, they react to a recommended advertisement or commercial as if they were typical of the audience to whom it is meant to appeal. But that is seldom the case.

An example of an advertisement that gives significance to a percentage, that was properly appreciated by the advertiser and that attracted a large number of prospects is on the following page. It was created by Grey Advertising and enthusiastically approved by Bank of America. (More about this ad in the case history at the end of this chapter.)

A personal example: While I was with Doremus & Company and faced the problem of how to give emotional significance to a table of repayment rates for home refinancing loans, I suggested ''When you borrow from the Dime, you can make the monthly payments as low as you wish if you own a home.'' As a result, large numbers of people visited the bank's branches saying they had seen the ad and wished to borrow money in the way described.

Advertising for banks, investment firms, and insurance companies is also made more difficult by the extraordinary number and variety of products and services whose sales can be increased through advertising. A partial list for commercial banks and investment firms is on page 9. For each of these products and services, a specific strategy needs to be developed. The proper audience must be defined, demographically and psychologically. The needs of the audiences must be discovered and understood, and the way the service or product can fulfill those needs must be developed and dramatized. What other industry must cope with such an array of products and services!

Mutual savings banks, savings and loan associations, and insurance companies don't offer so many services as commercial banks and investment firms do–not yet. But restrictions on what savings institutions can do are being lifted, and insurance companies are moving more and more into other areas of finance. In time, the services and products they advertise may approximate those of commercial banks and investment firms.

The continual introduction of new services alone would make financial advertising more difficult than most other types of advertising. Most other adver-

INTRODUCING A CHECKING ACCOUNT THAT PAYS LIKE AN INVESTMENT.

TRADE UP TO NEW INVESTORS CHECKING SERVICE AND TOP THE NOW ACCOUNTS.
8.29% TODAY'S ANNUAL YIELD†
8.00% TODAY'S RATE††

It's time to trade up. Up to new Investors Checking Service at Bank of America. If you keep a checking balance of $2,500 or more, this variable rate interest checking account is designed for you. Investors Checking Service gives you all the advantages of a regular interest-earning checking account, yet pays higher interest. Higher than the NOW accounts.* It's the highest earning interest checking account we offer. And unlike the "sweep" accounts, your entire Investors Checking account balance will earn the same higher interest when you maintain a $2,500 minimum daily balance. In addition, your entire balance (up to $100,000) is insured by the FDIC.

Besides higher interest, Investors Checking Service also gives you the ease and convenience of banking at over 1,000 Bank of America branches and over 400 VERSATELLER® machines. Plus you'll get unlimited check-writing privileges and your checks enjoy statewide recognition. You will receive our easy-to-read Timesaver Statement® and free personalized special checks. And, there are no monthly service charges for accounts with balances over $5,000.

FREE CREDIT CARD BONUS.

If you open an Investors Checking account by March 31, 1983, we'll give you an exciting bonus. Just bring in the coupon below for a bonus credit on any existing or new Bank of America credit card account you have.** You can even get this bonus on our most prestigious card, the BankAmericard® VISA® premium card. The premium card gives you a $5,000 line of credit, emergency cash and VISA Worldwide Traveler Service. Plus special high limit check cashing privileges at any Bank of America branch in California.

If you regularly maintain high checking balances, Investors Checking Service is made for you. In addition, Bank of America has a full range of checking plans to suit other needs. Either way, come talk with a Bank of America Financial Service Officer today.

BANK ON THE LEADER

BANK OF AMERICA

• BANK OF AMERICA. NT&SA 1983 • MEMBER FDIC

†After your interest is credited each month, you earn interest on it as well as on the principal. The yield assumes that the interest rate remains constant over one year and that deposits and interest remain in the account for a year. ††Rate may change daily. *$2,500 minimum deposit. If any daily balance falls below $2,500, the rate is 5¼% for the entire statement period. This account is available for balances up to $1,000,000. Certain restrictions may apply to deposits which would cause the balance to exceed $100,000. Call Bank of America for details. **VISA premium, VISA or MasterCard® credit cards. Bonus offer on new credit card accounts subject to application approval. ***This offer and coupon are subject to restrictions, exact coupon value is determined by type of credit card account. Refer to the Investors Checking Service Bonus Coupon Rules, and terms of the Investors Checking Service.

Some Advertisable Services

Commercial Banks	Investment Firms
Checking accounts	Common stocks
Savings accounts	Preferred stocks
Money market accounts	Corporate bonds
Certificates of deposit	Municipal bonds
Commercial loans	Municipal funds
Home mortgages	Unit trusts
Automobile loans	Mortgage-backed securities
General consumer loans	Commodity futures
Investment management	Financial futures
Discount brokerage	U.S. government securities
Asset-based financing	Real estate investment trusts
Wills	Real estate tax shelters
Estate management	Oil & gas tax shelters
Living trusts	Cattle & other types of tax shelters
Individual retirement accounts	Options
CMA-type accounts	Keogh plans
Leveraged lease financing	Individual retirement accounts
Safe deposit boxes	Annuities
Gold	Investment management
Super NOW accounts	CMA-type accounts
	New issues
	Secondary offerings
	Leveraged lease financing
	Custodial services
	Block trading
	Market making
	Precious metals

tising consists of giving new creative treatments to established products, but financial advertisers and their agencies continually move into unexplored territories—which is dangerous, no matter how much research is done beforehand.

For example, when Merrill Lynch launched its now so successful CMA (Cash Management Account), the commercials, advertisements, and direct mail concentrated on the concrete benefits to investors—mostly that investors get concise monthly reports on all their investments. This seems sensible, but the advertising was not successful, and the whole project would have been abandoned if top management had not had faith in the project and been willing to persevere, risking millions of dollars. Eventually, it was found that appealing to pride, emphasizing the prestige of a CMA account, worked best. And the advertising was successful from then on.

Financial advertisers generally cannot compete so strongly as other kinds of advertisers. Smaller banks, such as California First, may be able to use comparative advertising effectively, as the case history following Chapter 3 shows, but bigger banks usually cannot be so forceful. The reason: Their competitors are often also customers or allies. Money center banks provide a number of services to smaller banks, and banks often band together to make sizable loans, such as loans to foreign countries. Similarly, larger investment firms provide services to smaller firms, and investment firms continually unite to underwrite securities.

Insurance companies that sell fire and casualty insurance through their own sales forces compete fiercely with those that sell insurance through independent agents—but between insurance companies that sell the same way, the infighting tends to be gentlemanly because insurance companies often reinsure their big risks with other insurance companies.

Besides often being unable to be highly competitive, financial advertisements cannot exaggerate the way ads for other types of products can. A toothpaste or deodorant commercial can show girls swooning over a man because he uses the advertised product, but financial advertising must be more factual and realistic.

A highly successful creator of non-financial advertising once said that his formula was "Find a distinctive benefit and exaggerate the hell out of it!" But creators of financial advertising need to be more careful.

The U.S. Supreme Court has condoned "legal puffery" for non-financial advertising, but no such license is allowed financial advertisers. For example, a discount broker at one time intentionally set its schedule of brokerage commissions at a level believed by its marketing people to be lower than anybody else's. But the advertising could not contain a flat statement to that effect because the firm couldn't prove that somewhere there wasn't a firm that charged lower commissions. The discount broker was forced to put the competitive statement in the form of an opinion: "*We believe* we save investors more money than any other brokerage firm"—considerably weaker than "Nobody, but nobody, undersells Gimbels."

Of the three types of financial advertising—bank, insurance, investment—the most heavily regulated is investment advertising. Investment advertisers must contend with a thicket of regulations by the Securities and Exchange Commission (SEC), the National Association of Securities Dealers, the various stock and commodity exchanges, and sometimes other federal and state agencies.

In addition, investment advertisers and their agencies need to know not only the regulations but also how they are interpreted. Regulators interpret the laws and regulations differently at different times. In the 1950s, if a mutual fund had placed the forceful kind of advertising that is commonplace in the 1980s, the fund would soon have found itself put out of business by the Securities and Exchange Commission. Yet the law has not changed.

These fluctuations in interpretations make lawyers cautious, and the creator of advertising for one investment firm may find himself or herself forbidden to create advertising that another firm's lawyers would approve.

While fewer regulations affect bank and insurance advertising, advertisers in these industries and their agencies must be sure that nothing in their advertising could possibly be misleading. If it is, the company could be sued for fraud. In fact, if it could be, it *will* be sued.

There are sound reasons why the liberties common in other kinds of advertising cannot—and should not—be taken in financial advertising. Most other advertising polices itself, financial advertising cannot. Suppose, for example, a deodorant fails to perform as the buyer expected. All that the purchaser has lost is the price of one can. Another brand can be bought, and in addition to not buying the same brand again, the unhappy purchaser will tell friends. So non-financial advertising that features a benefit that the product does not have will draw attention to the absence of the benefit and sales will plummet.

Not so with most financial services. First the sums involved are seldom trivial. Instead of $2.98, a financial decision usually involves hundreds or thousands of dollars. And here's what really counts: The lack of a benefit falsely promised in a financial advertisement can seldom be perceived immediately. The benefits— interest, dividends, insurance payments—will all be received in the future, sometimes many years later. Misleading financial advertising is not immediately self-defeating.

So the regulations and the restraints in financial advertising are necessary, but they do contribute to the difficulties of creating the most effective advertising.

Yet the handicaps we have discussed so far—the abstract nature of the subject; the fact that the benefits are often being communicated most precisely in percentages or other numbers, whose significance cannot be readily grasped by readers, viewers and listeners; the large number of services involved; the continual introduction of new services; and the regulations and other restraints—all combined do not reduce the effectiveness of financial advertising as much as the last handicap we will discuss: Functionally, *financial advertising consists not merely of one kind of advertising but of several*, each of which must follow different principles for maximum success. And these principles often *directly conflict* with the *most commonly accepted principles* of advertising, which are founded on advertising for package goods.

Five kinds of advertising used to promote banks, investment firms, insurance companies, and nearly all their services are:

1. *Image advertising*. This kind of advertising aims to increase awareness of the advertiser and its services and to improve the attitudes of audiences toward the advertiser and its services.

2. *Direct response advertising*. This kind of advertising succeeds only if it causes viewers, readers or listeners to act immediately—usually to telephone or send in a coupon.

3. *Retail advertising*. This kind of advertising succeeds only if it causes prospects to visit the place of business of the advertiser. In this book it's called visit-our-office advertising to distinguish it from department store advertising.

4. *Reminder advertising*. This kind of advertising is closely allied to image advertising, but its principal purpose is simply to inform, that is, to tell readers, viewers, and listeners that the company exists and where to obtain its services when those services are desired. It does not aim to arouse emotion.

5. *Dealer-support advertising*. Some of those who sell the services of a bank, investment firm, or insurance company—firms, and independent insurance agents—are only loosely tied to the providers of the services they sell. They are audiences that need to be considered when any advertising is created and placed. Often they are one of the principal audiences of what appears to be consumer advertising.

Well-meaning articles in influential publications read by advertising people often add to the confusion about the principles that financial advertising must follow. Most of the articles concern package goods advertising—or are by people experienced only in package goods advertising—because most of the money spent on advertising promotes package goods. The writers of these articles often don't have enough varied experience to realize that the principles they expound do not apply to other types of advertising.

Many years ago, Young & Rubicam recognized that the principles of direct response advertising differ radically from those upon which Young & Rubicam had built its reputation and made it one of the largest agencies in the world: package goods advertising. Instead of trying to rationalize the differences between the various functional types, the agency took the pragmatic step of acquiring one of the most successful direct response agencies—Wunderman, Ricotta & Kline. When Young & Rubicam acquired the Merrill Lynch account in the 1970s, the parent company placed the television and other image advertising, while Wunderman, Ricotta & Kline created and placed the direct response advertising. Other general agencies, both before and after Young & Rubicam's action, have taken the same pragmatic step.

Citicorp and some other advertisers have adapted in a different way, retaining different agencies for different objectives, market methods, and services. In the early 1980s, Citicorp had 11 different agencies.

Most financial advertisers, however, do not have advertising budgets that are big enough to attract large, diversified agencies such as Young & Rubicam, nor are their budgets large enough to be split among two or more agencies. Divided, each account would be less profitable to each agency, and therefore, other things being equal, their agencies would not be able to attract and hold sufficiently talented creative and account people.

Further, educating one agency in the many services and peculiarities of financial advertising is hard enough without finding and educating two or more.

Consequently, most financial advertisers and their agencies need to understand (1) the principles of the several kinds of advertising used to increase the revenues of financial organizations and (2) how those principles differ from the principles we all read and hear most about—the principles of package goods advertising. Only when these principles and differences are understood can media people apply their knowledge intelligently, can creative people apply their ingenuity fruitfully, can account people recommend what is sound, and can advertisers judge what will be most profitable.

To indicate the validity and application of these principles, case histories appear periodically throughout this book. The case history that follows here tells more about the Investors Checking campaign and shows how many of the handicaps under which financial advertising labors can be overcome.

A SUPER NOW ACCOUNT BY ANY OTHER NAME CAN SEEM SWEETER

In December 1982, Federal regulators stunned the banking industry with an unexpected announcement: Beginning January 5, 1983, banks and savings and loan companies could for the first time offer Super NOW checking—an interest-paying checking service with no prescribed interest rate ceiling.

The announcement's timing could not have been worse—just one month after banks and savings and loans had introduced their first money market fund accounts. As a result, Super NOW checking debuted in an advertising arena already crowded with competitive money market campaigns by banks, savings and loans, brokerage houses, and thrifts.

For Grey Advertising Inc., Bank of America's agency, the challenge was to find a way to immediately put their client in the forefront of the Super NOW category. To do so, advertising would need to establish Bank of America's Super NOW account as (1) different from other Bank of America services and (2) preferable to Super NOW accounts offered by competitive financial institutions.

The key to success lay in translating the interest-paying benefit into a fresh, succinct phrase—"A checking account that pays like an investment"— and giving the account a distinctive name embodying the benefit: "Investors Checking." Thus Bank of America's Super NOW accounts were set apart from other Super NOW accounts, which were promoted on the basis of high interest rates stated in numbers. Further, the phrase "Investors Checking" had upscale connotations, which increased the appeal through identification.

Newspapers, television, radio, direct mail, and a lobby poster were used, as well as an incentive plan for the bank's employees. The newspaper advertisements were either full-page or of dominating size. (One is shown, reduced, earlier in this chapter.) They appeared twice in the first week and weekly thereafter for the first three months. Television was used during the second month only, radio during the second and third months.

The newspaper ads used the campaign's key phrase as the headline and immediately stated the yield in numbers for accurate substantiation. The copy gave more benefits and concluded with an incentive to act promptly.

The television and radio commercials were set in a stockbrokerage office (complete with anxious tote board viewers) to stress and dramatize the investment theme. This setting also made it easy to reenforce the safety associated with banks in contrast to the risk associated with brokerage firms. This attribute may have helped return to banks dollars that had been lost to brokerage money market funds.

1.   1st MAN: One day you're up, one day you're down.

2.   2nd MAN: You never know.

3.   3rd MAN: Thank goodness for my checking account.

4.   2nd MAN: Since when is a checking account an investment?

5.   3rd MAN: Since they got Bank of America's Investors Checking

6.   It pays like an investment.

7.   Works like a regular checking account.

8.   2nd MAN: It tops my NOW account.

9.   1st MAN: It tops my whole portfolio.

10.   3rd MAN: And it's insured.

11.   ANNCR: New Investors Checking Service; it pays like an investment.

12.   (MUSIC) CHORUS: Bank on the leader. Bank of America. (MUSIC OUT)

Investors Checking TV Commercial (30 seconds)

Investors Checking Radio Commercial (one minute)

BUSINESS SFX:	Typewriters, etc.
MAN 1:	(Confused) What's going on with the stock market?
MAN 2:	(Sounding dismayed) One day you're up, one day you're down.
MAN 1:	You never know.
MAN 3:	Thank goodness for my checking account.
MAN 1:	Since when is a checking account an investment?
MAN 3:	Since Bank of America introduced new Investors Checking Service. It pays like an investment but works like a regular checking account.
MAN 1:	Pays like an *investment*?? A *checking* account??
MAN 3:	That's right. Take a look.
MAN 2:	Tops my NOW account.
MAN 1:	Tops my whole portfolio!
MAN 3:	And it's insured.
MAN 1 & 2:	(In unison) Insured?
SFX:	PEOPLE RUNNING FOR DOORS
MAN 1:	(Fading over SFX) Wait for me . . . !
MAN 3:	Where's everybody going?
ANNCR:	Bank of America's new Investors Checking Service, the checking account that pays like an investment. Open your account by March 31st and ask about our Bank of America credit card bonus.
MUSIC:	LEADER THEME
ANNCR:	Member FDIC. Minimum balance $2,500. Restrictions may apply to accounts over $100,000.
LIVE TAG:	Rate effective ——— is ———%. Rate may change daily.

Thanks to Grey's strong, thoughtful, and creative effort, Investors Checking Service became an immediate, outstanding success. Within three months of introduction, Bank of America held a 48.5% share of Super NOW dollars and a 46.7% share of Super NOW accounts among California's top five banks (more than double the bank's historic 20% share of regular NOW accounts). What is more, the average balance per account was high—62% higher than had been anticipated.

HOW A NEWLY FORMED INSURANCE AND FINANCIAL SERVICES COMPANY ESTABLISHED A FAVORABLE IMAGE FAST

"CIGNA" was a new name in the insurance and financial services industry in 1982. Formed by the merger of Connecticut General Corporation and INA Corporation, leading providers of employee benefits and property/casualty insurance, CIGNA Corporation needed to create awareness of its new name and establish a quality image among the following audiences:

- Senior management of companies ranging from owners of small businesses up to and including Fortune 1000 companies
- Insurance decision makers in the Fortune 1000 companies
- Affluent individuals (annual incomes of over $55,000)
- Independent *insurance* agents *and brokers.*

CIGNA'S ad agency, Doyle Dane Bernbach Group Inc., recommended dividing a $7.5 million budget about evenly between print ads and television commercials. The print media chosen consisted of *The Wall Street Journal, Forbes, Fortune, BusinessWeek,* and other business and trade magazines. Ads were scheduled to be seen at least three times per quarter by target audiences.

The ads and commercials won awards in virtually every major awards contest.

The ads focused on problems currently being faced by the target audiences, but did so in dramatic, tasteful, and often humorous ways. The ads were not depressing. Instead, they were supportive, offering CIGNA'S solutions to the problems.

One ad featured the Roman Coliseum in its current decayed state. The headline was "In America, the architect could still be held liable for it." Another showed an old man getting food stamps. The headline was "For Some Retired People, Stamp Collecting Isn't a Hobby." Even if readers went no further than the illustration, headline, and signature, the advertisements conveyed the strong impression that CIGNA companies help businesses handle their problems.

The Wall Street Journal measured the readership of three of the ads by a technique similar to that used by Daniel Starch and Staff. All the measured ads had similar scores and turned out to be the three best-read insurance ads measured by *The Wall Street Journal* during 1983.

Two television spots, placed on a continuing basis on news and news analysis shows, and periodically on telecasts of tennis and golf events, took a broader creative approach, using humor to maintain interest and to cause the name "CIGNA" to be remembered. One focused on INA's activities, the other on Connecticut General's.

WILL IT COME TO THIS?

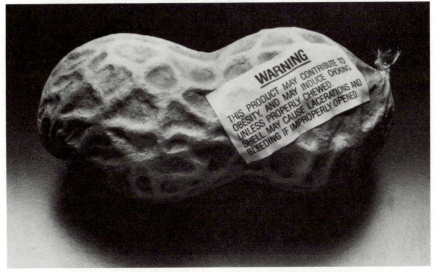

WARNING
THIS PRODUCT MAY CONTRIBUTE TO OBESITY, AND MAY INDUCE CHOKING. UNLESS PROPERLY CHEWED. SHELL MAY CAUSE LACERATIONS AND BLEEDING IF IMPROPERLY OPENED.

Warnings have come a long way since someone had the good sense to put a ☠ on an iodine bottle.

Courts now require warning labels on a whole range of products.

From paint thinner to pajamas.

There have also been rulings on exactly how large such labels should be. And where they should be.

And what they should say.

And it hasn't stopped at labeling, either.

Requirements relating to all aspects of product safety have mushroomed in recent years.

And while these have been a benefit to consumers, they've often been a problem for manufacturers.

Because even a responsible corporation can face liability by unintentionally overlooking a new regulation or an obscure ruling.

That's why at INA, a CIGNA company, we're prepared to do more than just insure our clients against product liability.

We do everything we can to keep them out of court.

To start with, we have a staff of product lia-bility specialists who can examine every step in the manufacturing and marketing process.

From product design to advertising.

And we're not only likely to spot weak-nesses people within a company may over-look, we're also more likely to spot weaknesses general and less specialized loss control examiners might overlook, as well.

We even look for problems before they occur.

We'll help design a product recall pro-gram, for example, to have in place, ready to quickly implement if the need for it ever arises.

And, needless to say, on an ongoing basis, we monitor legislation, court rulings, and agency regulations that can affect our client's liability.

If you'd like more information on this topic, please write to INA at 1600 Arch Street, Dept. RA, Philadelphia, Pennsylvania 19101.

Or, if you'd like to know how we can help protect you against product liability exposures, call your agent or broker.

After all, in an area as complicated as this one it's entirely possible a consumer isn't the only one who can benefit from a warning.

Insurance Company of North America
a CIGNA company

WHY SHOULD HE CARE WHAT IT COSTS? THE COMPANY'S BUYING.

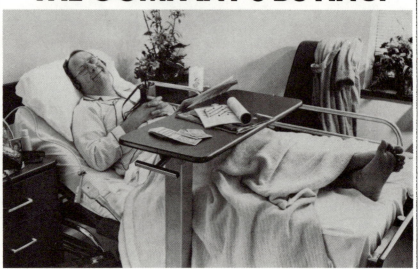

Expense account psychology isn't limited to executive lunches.

It is, unfortunately, alive and well in employees who find themselves ill.

And a corporation's best laid plans for containing medical costs often don't stand a chance against, "I'm covered for it."

With this in mind, we at Connecticut General, a CIGNA company, approach the issue of rising medical costs not only as a financial problem, but as an educational one.

It isn't enough, for example, to offer a second opinion on elective surgery.

Or one-day surgery.

Or pre-admission testing.

Employees have to know these things are available.

Even a high deductible and co-payment aren't enough. Because all they supply is an incentive to reduce costs, not the means.

So we provide brochures, mailers, promotional material, videotapes, and advise our clients on how to use these to motivate their employees.

Not surprisingly, we've discovered that most employees don't realize there are alternatives to long hospital stays.

When it's feasible, many would prefer a nurse at home to a week in the hospital.

And when they're offered, many are also willing to take advantage of preventive medicine programs such as blood pressure screening.

We're not suggesting that employee education is the single answer to this serious problem.

In fact, our programs cover a range of approaches. From funding business coalitions working to reduce local costs, to providing companies with data to track the effectiveness of their own cost containment activities.

But it remains true that even a plan as sophisticated as our cost containment package can't be completely effective unless employees are involved in the effort.

So if you'd like more information about reducing group medical expenses, please write to Connecticut General, Dept. A-141-A, Hartford, Connecticut 06152.

Or if you'd like to know how we can specifically help reduce your company's costs, please call your broker or your local Connecticut General representative.

After all, this may well be an area in which management could benefit from a little education, itself.

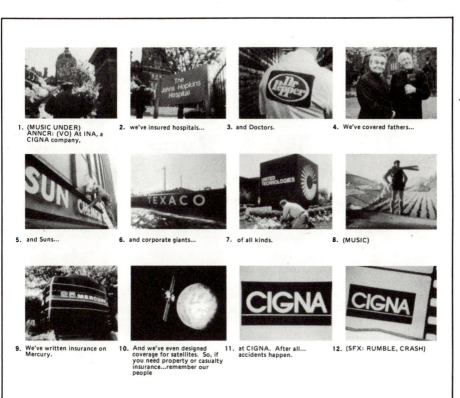

1. (MUSIC UNDER) ANNCR: (VO) At INA, a CIGNA company,
2. we've insured hospitals...
3. and Doctors.
4. We've covered fathers...
5. and Suns...
6. and corporate giants...
7. of all kinds.
8. (MUSIC)
9. We've written insurance on Mercury.
10. And we've even designed coverage for satellites. So, if you need property or casualty insurance...remember our people
11. at CIGNA. After all... accidents happen.
12. (SFX: RUMBLE, CRASH)

CIGNA TV Commercial (30 seconds)

A few advertisements, placed in publications read by independent insurance agents, told how CIGNA companies were helping independent agents survive by reducing their costs and helping them sell.

Surveys taken of insurance decision-makers, brokers, and independent agents in Fall 1982 and a year later showed awareness of the CIGNA name increasing from 37% in Fall 1982 to 72% in Fall 1983, even though the advertising did not start appearing until March 1983.

The campaign far exceeded its objectives, in addition to generating a record number of requests for reprints of ads and more information. Only strong, emotion-arousing ads could have so pierced the insurance boredom barrier.

WHICH DISCOUNT BROKERAGE AD PULLED BETTER?

As the first step in our discussion of a direct response advertising, look over the advertisements on the following pages. Both ads appeared in *The New*

You can save $1225.80 a year in brokerage commissions

Suppose you purchase 300 shares of a stock priced at $20 per share. The old fixed rate was $116.74. Our rate is 70% lower. You pay us only $35.02. You save $81.72 on this trade. Do that 15 times a year and you save $1225.80 a year.

Actually you **save even more** if you are now using Merrill Lynch, Dean Witter, Bache or any other full price broker. They've raised their commissions up to 20% or more above the old fixed rates.

What is more, comparisons show **we save investors more money than any discount broker.** That's because we charge not "up to" but a flat 70% off on all stock trades, with a $30 minimum. There are no gimmicks or time limitations. Nor is our rate schedule rigged so you get a big discount on the type of trade you never make but less than 50% discount on the type of trade you always make. When we're your broker, you never get less than 70% off.

We're able to save investors more while executing orders with the same expertise as any full price broker for several reasons. Three are paramount:

1. The orders you place with us are executed by our own brokers on the floor of the New York Stock Exchange, of which we are members. Most other discount brokers are primarily order takers. (Some are not even members of the New York Stock Exchange.) They must go to some other firm to have their orders executed.

2. We not only execute your orders, we "clear" them as well. ("Clearing" is the technical term for the record-keeping, mailing of confirmations and statements, etc.) Most other discount brokers, even those who are members of the New York Stock Exchange, have their orders cleared by some other firm. We are able to save on the execution and on the clearing. (Besides being 100% responsible for every order from beginning to end.)

3. We believe we are the largest discount broker. We have more capital than any other discount broker, the records

show. We exceeded the one billion dollar mark in yearly volume of trading some time ago. We pass along to you the cost efficiencies possible only in a large firm.

There are other advantages, besides saving money, for making us your broker. The confirmations and statements you receive will be *accurate* because we, from the top management down, specialize in processing and executing orders; we don't give investment advice. You get courteous, reliable service—all our Professional Traders are fully qualified representatives of the New York Stock Exchange. You'll get fast answers to questions about your account because we have all the information handy in our own possession, unlike discount brokers who don't do their own clearing. Plus, free delivery of your securities. Or, if you wish, free safekeeping.

We're members of the Securities Investor Protection Corporation. And because of our sizable capital—several times higher than the legal requirement—your money is protected even more.

Opening an account is easy. You don't even need to visit our firm, although you're more than welcome.

We'll be glad to send you a Schedule which makes obvious precisely how much you save on a specific purchase or sale. Just mail the coupon or telephone today. You'll also receive a free brochure which tells more about us and the forms for opening an account.

Phone toll-free (800)   except in New York State call collect (212)

Big Savings on Options and Bonds As Well.

On options you pay only half the old fixed rates established by the Chicago Board Options Exchange. On both corporate and municipal bonds you pay only $2.50 per $1000 bond with a $30 minimum per transaction.

Name of Discount Broker
Address

Please send me, free and without obligation, your **70% Off Commission Schedule**, free brochure, and forms for opening an account. I understand no salesman will call.

Name _____

Address _____

City_____ State _____ Zip_____

21

York Times in the Sunday financial section. An A–B split was used, that is, the ads appeared in alternate editions of the paper on the same day. The ads were a quarter page in size, because this is the minimum size The New York Times would accept for A–B split testing. There is little difference in the copy. The agency was Benn & MacDonough, Inc.

The answer to which pulled better is contained in the next chapter.

2

FINANCIAL DIRECT RESPONSE ADVERTISING

Of the several functional kinds of insurance used by banks, investment firms, and insurance companies, the principles of direct response advertising are the most firmly established. We can be surer of them than of the guidelines established for other kinds of advertising, because the results of a direct response ad or commercial are immediately and directly measurable.

For decades, direct response advertisers have been counting coupons, telephone calls, and orders received from different media, from different creative approaches, from different-size advertisements, establishing hypotheses and testing them again and again.

Image advertising, in contrast, depends upon surveys for measurement, but surveys are less exact and less reliable. Further, the effects of image advertising are long-term, and the results may be affected by something other than advertising—public relations, for example.

Next to direct response advertising, we know the principles of package goods advertising best—partly because the effect of the advertising on sales can be measured within a short period after the advertising appears, partly because so much money has been spent testing ways to increase sales.

In this chapter, the principles of package goods advertising—which many assume to apply to all advertising—will be contrasted with the principles of direct response advertising.

The difference between successful direct response advertising and successful package goods advertising derives mostly from the difference in their purposes. The aim of most package goods advertising aims to influence a shopper in the choice of a brand. When the shopper enters a supermarket she (or he) already knows what she needs—for example, paper towels. The purpose of Bounty's advertising is to cause her to choose Bounty instead of Scott or some other brand.

And this choice is made some time, perhaps several days, after she has seen the commercial. Consequently, package goods advertising must, above all, cause viewers, readers and listeners to *remember*.

Copywriters and art directors are continually developing ways to make the name of the product and the benefit associated with it memorable. The techniques may arouse a deep emotion, such as fear (as in the "ring-around-the-collar" commercials) or the name of the product and its benefits may be encompassed in a song. Humor may be used. Everybody likes to remember something funny.

Memory experts have determined that one way to remember something is to tie it in closely with something else already known. The Bounty commercials do this by featuring a celebrity, Nancy Walker. Memory is also enhanced through repetition, so the name Bounty is repeated several times in the commercial, and the commercial itself is repeated often.

A direct response advertisement or commercial, in contrast, does not need to be memorable at all. Its aim is to get immediate action, not to affect a delayed choice. A direct response advertisement or commercial therefore concentrates on arousing the desire of readers, viewers, or listeners—on making them want what is being offered. The most successful direct response advertisements and commercials usually arouse desire by beginning with a benefit. The copy may then go on to make the benefit even more mouth-watering—to name additional benefits, clear away objections, and to tell the readers, viewers, or listeners what they must do to get the benefit(s).

Getting immediate action is difficult. The few words or few words and picture(s) in an advertisement or commercial must cause readers, viewers, or listeners to telephone immediately or tear out the coupon and fill it in immediately—or at least make a note to do so soon. And if the coupon is sent in, they have still more trouble. A pen, an envelope, and a stamp must be found, and the envelope has to be addressed and mailed.

So the benefit offered in a direct response commercial or advertisement must be strong. Of course, it is desirable that the benefit in a package goods commercial be strong, but often it's not essential. The shopper is going to buy the product anyway. So just a small difference can cause the shopper to buy one brand instead of another. If scales are evenly balanced, a slight touch can depress one side, elevate the other.

Package goods advertising is concerned with brand differentiation. Direct response advertising is concerned with product desire. That's the chief reason why the discount brokerage advertisement with the headline "You can save $1225.80 a year in brokerage commissions" outpulled "We believe we can save investors more money than any other discount broker." The "$1225.80 a year" headline aroused desire. The "save investors more money" mostly differentiated the advertiser from other discount brokers.

Besides differing in their beginnings and middles, package goods advertising and direct response advertising differ in their endings. Successful package goods commercials and ads usually end with a prominent logo or picture of the package, because that's what the audience must remember if the advertising is to be successful. In direct response advertising, the ending endeavors to increase responses by urging respondents to act immediately, giving them a reason for so doing if possible, and making it easy for them to respond promptly by including a coupon, address, and/or telephone number.

Humor is seldom successful in direct response advertising. Humor relieves anxiety. After hearing a joke, one leans back, satisfied—just as at the end of a hearty dinner. In contrast, direct response must cause people to want something, to be hungry.

Successful direct response advertising also deviates from generally accepted advertising principles in the matter of frequency. To illustrate, we'll use another discount brokerage example because it uniquely illustrates the differences between package goods and direct response advertising in a practical way.

A group of marketing consultants to package goods companies, such as Proctor & Gamble, decided to go into the discount brokerage business on their own. They had already successfully established several small businesses. These were experienced, intelligent men.

They chose as the advertising agency for their discount brokerage company an agency in which they had confidence because of its success with package goods. The agency made the mistake of creating an ad featuring a weak comparative benefit: the higher insurance the discount brokerage firm had on money and securities held by the firm for customers.

The ad pulled very poorly the first few times it appeared. But neither the agency nor the owners of the discount brokerage firm were discouraged. From their experience with package goods advertising, they believed that a certain amount of repetition is necessary until the advertising would have an effect. Shoppers need to see package good advertising again and again so that they will remember the product and the advertised comparative benefit when they go to the supermarket.

The advertiser was so convinced that repetition was necessary that more than a million dollars was spent on the advertising, without success! Then the operating head of the discount brokerage firm consulted Benn & MacDonough. At a meeting with the owners of the firm, they heard why repetition was not necessary—that a direct response advertisement in print either pulls well the first time or it won't pull at all.

An ad was created for them with a strong benefit in the headline:

Now!
A Discount Broker
That Supplies You with
The Information You Need
+
Commission Savings
of Up to 80%!

This headline promised many investors what they wanted. The advertisement pulled very, very well on the first insertion in *The Wall Street Journal*. By the way, the headline could have been run by competing brokers because, as the copy made clear, the information was furnished by sending investors a Standard & Poor's report on any of several thousand stocks—something that any discount broker could do at little cost, and that many did do but did not advertise.

Package goods commercials and advertisements need to be repeated close together so that the brand and its benefit are indelibly imprinted on prospects' minds. But this is not necessary with direct response advertisements. To be successful, the prospect must act immediately or the advertisement is a failure.

In fact, repeating a direct response advertisement too soon can be a waste of money. If the first ad is very successful and draws replies from a higher percentage of true prospects, fewer are left for the second ad to convince. To take an extreme example, suppose a direct response money market advertisement took up a whole page in a newspaper, and then the same ad was repeated the next day. Obviously the second ad would pull fewer responses because most interested readers of the newspaper would have responded to the first ad.

TV and radio commercials differ somewhat from print ads in the matter of repetition. Commercials may need to be repeated so that listeners and viewers will remember the telephone number or address given in the commercial. But the required repetition is nowhere near so extensive as in package goods marketing. Some experience indicates that replies from a one-minute radio commercial placed on the same program every day increase until about the third day, and then slowly decline.

Direct response and package goods advertising differ in the matter of length. Thirty seconds, perhaps even 15 seconds, is fine for a package goods TV commercial because memorability counts most. A single memorable concept can be communicated in that time. Direct response TV commercials and advertisements may need to be longer because the viewer must be convinced and motivated to act immediately, and giving the phone number and/or address takes time.

Consequently, most successful direct response TV commercials are sometimes much longer than the standard 30 seconds—some are as long as 2 minutes. The length of the ad or commercial depends upon the complexity of the product or service, the logical and emotional objections that need to be overcome, how much the target audience already knows about the product or service, and what respondents are expected to do.

Bank TV commercials can usually be shorter than investment commercials, because most banking services can be readily understood and there's little risk involved with banks. Insurance commercials usually need to be longest because much reluctance to buy must be overcome.

If respondents are asked to send for a free booklet, a TV commercial (or print ad) can be shorter than if the commercial (or ad) tries to make an immediate sale. It takes more urging to cause respondents to send in checks or have the cost applied to their credit cards.

For radio commercials, optimum frequency and length are slightly different. Keeping the attention of the audience on a single subject for more than a minute through the ears alone is difficult. Successful telemarketing scripts, for example, consist largely of short statements followed by questions to stimulate replies, because people are not apt to just listen for any length of time when they are being sold. For this reason, direct response radio commercials are usually only one minute long. Some repetition helps, not only for memorability of the telephone number and/or address but also for understanding. Readers of a print advertisement who don't immediately catch the meaning of a word, phrase, or sentence can always reread it. A well-written TV commercial communicates information both orally and visually, so that little misunderstanding is likely. But if listeners do not catch the meaning of part of a radio commercial immediately, they can't reread it.

No matter what the medium, the differences between the principles of direct response advertising and the generally accepted principles for all advertising, which are based on successes with package goods, are extensive and significant. A summary follows.

How the Principles of Package Goods and Direct Response Advertising Compare

	Package Goods	Direct Response
Objective	Memorability	Immediate action
Brand differentiation	Most important	Not important
Benefit	Slight may be OK	Strong necessary
Copy	Features mnemonic devices	Logical progression from benefit to action desired
Ending	Big logo or package	Facilitates action
Humor	Often successful	Seldom successful
Length of commercial	Standard OK	Extra length may be necessary
Repetition of ad or commercial	Essential	Not necessary for print, modest for TV & radio

SMALL ADS FOR BOND INSURANCE PULL RESPONSES AT LOW COST

In 1980, municipal bond insurance was relatively new. Many bond professionals felt it was unnecessary and termed it "overkill." The Municipal Bond Insurance Association (MBIA), of which Paul O'Shea was advertising manager, decided to embark on an advertising campaign whose primary objective was to inform investors and professional municipal bond people of the advantages of MBIA-insured municipal bonds. The advertising was also a test to see (1) how great (or little) the interest in bond insurance was, (2) how effective (or ineffective) advertising on this unglamorous subject could be, and (3) which media would be best for municipal bond insurance advertising.

Small one-column advertisements were created by MBIA's advertising agency, Benn & MacDonough, and placed in *The New York Times*, the *Miami Herald*, the *Los Angeles Times*, *The Wall Street Journal*, *Barron's*, and *U.S. News & World Report*. The ads offered a free booklet.

The responses were far greater than the most optimistic forecast—more than triple the number that would have justified the program—and some of the responses were for multiple copies of the booklet. Citibank requested 2500 to send to high-income clients.

(Actual size)

(Actual size)

The average cost per response was much lower than anticipated—about $8.00. None of the media pulled badly, but, as had been anticipated by the agency, the media in which most of the money was expended, *The New York Times* and *The Wall Street Journal*, pulled replies at the lowest cost per response.

A survey taken of the respondents indicated that over half of the investors responding intended to buy MBIA-insured municipal bonds or already had.

As a partial consequence of the success of this advertising, MBIA undertook an extensive advertising campaign in succeeding years to promote the advantages of MBIA-insured municipal bonds. Soon MBIA, which had been second in dollar volume of municipal bonds insured, moved into first place.

DIRECT MAIL CAUSES OVER 100% OF DEALERS ADDRESSED TO PARTICIPATE IN AN AUTO LOAN PROGRAM

AmeriTrust had developed an automobile loan financing plan for dealers which AmeriTrust officials knew was superior to any plan currently being offered in the Cleveland area. But Cleveland automobile dealers obviously felt well-satisfied with their present financing programs. Something needed to be done that would make them listen.

The number of prospects was small—just 168 key dealers—so direct mail advertising was indicated. Three mailings were sent in November 1983.

The first mailing consisted of a paperback copy of the runaway number-one best-seller, *The One Minute Manager*, along with the letter on the following page.

Two or three days later the 168 prospects received a second mailing consisting of a canister of Hershey kisses, labeled "The One," accompanied by the next letter.

The third mailing, received after another two- or three-day interval, consisted of an orchid, labeled "The One," and the next letter.

The gifts were not just cute ideas to gain attention. Each gift emphasized the distinctive feature of AmeriTrust's loan program which would be of benefit to the dealers: a single interest rate regardless of the size or maturity of the loan. Note too that the letters did not try to be tricky, but directly and clearly explained the benefits to the dealer.

The mailings fitted the parameters. They took full advantage of the unique potentialities of the *medium*, they solved the problem posed by the attitude of the *audience* toward the *subject*, and they showed how much superior "The One" was to the *competition* (the dealers' present financing program). And everything was centered on the *purpose*—obtaining an appointment during which prospects would be not only attentive but pre-sold.

The result of the mailings and visits by sales representatives was that 166 out of the 168 dealers signed up for the AmeriTrust financing program. Many of those who became customers told other dealers, making a total of 208 who signed up—124% of the number mailed to!

THE ONE

The *one low rate* program
for dealers

November 10, 1983

Dear Mr. Jarrett:

We call it "The One."

It's our new and used car financing program.

It's a brand new and remarkably different program.

You'll like it.

That's because we offer you a single flat rate:

        for new cars

        for used cars

        for any and all maturities.

So you have one rate to work with.

And you have one low rate to give you lots of flexibility.

So you see why we call it "The One."

There's more to tell. We'll be in touch.

Enthusiastically,

Dick Wise
Vice President

DW/ybc
Enc.
P.S. The "One Minute Manager" is the one among today's
management books. It hit the best seller list with
one idea. A management idea that can be good for
your company and your bottom line. Same with our
plan. One idea, one low rate. And very good for
your bottom line. It's "The One."

AmeriTrust

4169 Pearl Road, Suite 200, Cleveland, Ohio 44101

THE ONE

The *one low rate* program
for dealers

November 14, 1983

Dear Mr. Jarrett:

Let me tell you more about our wonderful new, new and used
car financing program for dealers.

As you know, we call it "The One."

You get one flat rate to work with. 12.25 A.P.R. You can
use it for new cars and for used cars. For 24 months,
36 months or 48 months.

You can close a deal with your customer at 13.50 A.P.R.,
14.50 A.P.R. or even 14.75 A.P.R. I'm sure you'll admit
that spread will give you lots of flexibility.

Of course you know how a 12.25 A.P.R. "buy rate" will help
you with used car financing. It'll be a terrific tool.
And you know that a 12.25 A.P.R. is very, very competitive
for new cars, too.

I don't have to tell you that our one single rate will be
very easy to work with. Your people will be able to
figure alternate deals in a flash. For example, if you're
moving a customer from a new to used or a used to new car
deal, the rates will be identical, and the switch will be
easy.

Now let's consider your dealer reserve.

On a $7500 loan advance for 48 months you can earn from
$0-$450.00. You determine the amount you earn.

Compare these amounts to your present reserve, and you'll
see why "The One" program is the one for you.

AmeriTrust

4169 Pearl Road, Suite 200, Cleveland, Ohio 44101

There's more to tell, of course.

That's why I suggest you may want to call me at 216/351-1114.
I'm here to answer your questions.

I like to talk about it. I'm sure you can understand why.

Call me today,

Dick Wise
Vice President

DW/ybc
Enc.
P.S. Hershey is the one in chocolate. Success came from
      one idea. Produce a uniform, highest-quality product
      consistently year after year. Same with our plan.
      One idea, one uniform rate. It's "The One."

THE ONE

The *one low rate* program
for dealers

November 16, 1983

Dear Mr. Jarrett:

Among flowers, the orchid is "The One."

It has based its success on one idea. Superiority.

Our program follows the same approach. One idea, one rate,
a superior plan.

We think it's "The One."

We have designed our program to do a superior job for you.
Think about it. A 12.25 A.P.R. flat rate across the board
for new and used cars, and for all maturities from 12 to
48 months.

Consider what that will do for your salespeople. They'll
have a lot more flexibility; they'll find the rates easy
to figure; and they'll close more sales.

You'll have happier customers, too, because you'll be able
to make better deals.

We'll do our part also.

Our people are committed to serving you in the very best
way they know how. They have a good product and are
trained to help you with every detail.

We are set to give you immediate service. We have installed
the latest state of the art equipment in our offices to
enable us to give you fast approvals. And there's a neat
bonus plan, too.

4169 Pearl Road, Suite 200, Cleveland, Ohio 44101

34

I know you will want to hear the whole story. That's why
I have asked our representative to stop by to explain the
entire program. They'll give you a call first. They're
excited about it.

I know you will be, too.

                                     Sincerely,

                                     Dick Wise
                                     Vice President

DW/ybc
Enc.
P.S. I'm sure you know somebody who will truly appreciate
      the orchid. It's a Cattleya flown in especially for
      you.

The objective had been to make 1270 loans in three months, but in only half that time, 1621 loans were made, totaling over $10 million. For each $1000 invested in the mailings, almost $3 million in loans had resulted.

The agency, Yeck Brothers Group of Dayton, Ohio, was guided by AmeriTrust Vice President Richard Wise. A Silver Echo Award was received from the Direct Marketing Association.

HOW A NEW COMPANY BECAME THE HIGHEST REGARDED DEALER IN INVESTMENT DIAMONDS

In 1979, Norman Gross had proven himself to be an unusually capable entrepreneur and business manager. He had established a very profitable indoor tennis facility and organized it so well that it almost ran itself. He just needed to check on how it was operating from time to time.

Gross had picked the right time to start such a business, and now he looked around for another that might offer a similar timely opportunity. Inflation was a big worry in 1979, so he decided to go into the business of selling diamonds for investment.

He discussed the distinctive competitive benefit he had developed with me. (I was a customer of his tennis facility.) Benn & MacDonough researched the diamond business; wrote and designed a handsome, illustrated two-color brochure; and wrote, designed and placed the advertisement shown on the facing page. It appeared only in the Eastern edition of *The Wall Street Journal*.

Note that: (1) The illustration and headline would attract anyone interested in investing in diamonds. (2) The strong benefit is substantiated by the copy. (3) The copy is set in 8-point type, the coupon copy even smaller. (4) While the eyebrow headline insures that there will be numerous responses with the words, "Free brochure," the screen near the end of the copy, "Minimum investment: $4000," reduces the number and increases the quality.

Principally because of this ad and the booklet—and Norman Gross's acute business sense and salesmanship—Diamond Portfolio, Ltd., quickly became a profitable diamond dealing firm. Four years later, as a result of subsequent advertising and publicity that capitalized on developments in the investment diamond marketplace—plus Norman Gross's high moral character—Diamond Portfolio, Ltd., was described as "probably the best firm selling diamonds to the public" out of 142 companies surveyed by the well-respected *Gem Market Reporter.*

A DAVID-SIZED BLUE CROSS PLAN IS THROWN INTO COMPETITION WITH A GOLIATH

In 1983, the Virginia Assembly eliminated the boundaries that had separated and protected the marketing territory of Blue Cross and Blue Shield of Southwestern Virginia–Roanoke, from the marketing territory of a much larger, similar organization—Blue Cross and Blue Shield of Virginia, headquartered in Richmond.

How could the Roanoke-headquartered Plan compete? It had much smaller resources, fewer salespeople, one-fifth the enrollment, a smaller advertising budget, and a geographically restricting name. How could it prevent the bigger plan from gobbling it up?

The first step was defensive. In April, three months before the boundary would be eliminated, advertisements were placed in local newspapers within the Roanoke-based Plan's own territory with the following headline and subhead:

Our 1982 Rates
for Group Coverage
Were So Popular
We're Offering Them
Into 1984.

**If you act before May 27, 1983
we guarantee our 1982 rates for a full year.**

Several paragraphs of copy were followed by a large coupon and an illustration of a telephone with the words "Call toll-free in Virginia: 1–800–543–3200" in type as large as the subhead. As a result, group proposals leapt from 80 in the first quarter to 220 during the second quarter.

But what would happen when each association could invade the other's territory?

Vice President for Advertising, Andy Mayo, and Senior Vice President of Marketing, Frank Taylor of Blue Cross and Blue Shield of Southwestern Virginia, had some marketing research done which gave them a glimmer of hope. They discovered that Goliath was well-regarded but ranked low in flexibility and benefit design. Sales could be made if prospects could be found and talked to! But how could the Roanoke-based Plan be distinguished from its neighbor and the liability of the geographically restricting name be overcome? Even the symbols were identical. They handed the problem to Jerry Conrad, Senior Vice President of the Plan's advertising agency, Houck & Harrison.

After some deliberation, the agency recommended a solution that now seems obvious: emphasizing a memorable 800 telephone number instead of the Plan's name.

But before creating any advertising, the agency tried the concept out in focus group interviews with business leaders. The findings gave a go-ahead signal.

The largest segment of the nearly $500,000, three-month campaign was devoted to television. A month before the marketing boundary was eliminated, a 30-second commercial was placed on upper demographic shows so as to catch the attention of business decision-makers: golf and tennis events, public affairs, news shows, and news-type shows such as "60 Minutes" and "20/20." The commercial (shown on the opposite page), and other advertising, which won a Gold Effie from the American Marketing Association, was created by Tom Hale and Betse Feuchtenberger.

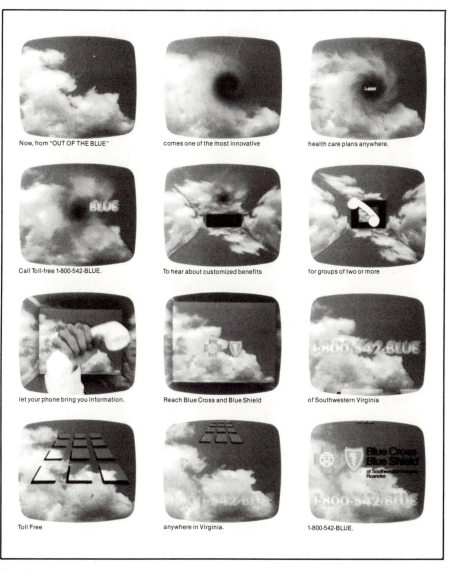

Blue Cross and Blue Shield of Southwestern Virginia TV Commercial (30 seconds)

Two weeks of television advertising, running alone, was followed by a week of radio scheduled almost entirely on travel, news, and sports programs during drive time.

Print and outdoor advertising followed, with the ads appearing in local newspapers and in local, statewide, and in-flight magazines. All the ads, even those in local newspapers, featured a background of blue sky and clouds. The print ads had this headline and subhead:

Now, From Out of the Blue,
Innovative Group Benefits
For All Virginia
1–800–542-BLUE

Call toll-free anywhere in Virginia to
discover what's new in Blue Cross and
Blue Shield benefits

The outdoor advertising, placed in highly industrialized areas, was similar. In big type over a blue sky with white clouds were the words

From Out of the Blue,
Group Health Benefits
For All Virginia
Call 1–800–542-BLUE

Below, much smaller, were the Blue Cross and Blue Shield symbols along with the association's name. "Of Southwestern Virginia" was even smaller in size.

Direct mail was also used, and vigorous publicity supported the entire effort.

To take advantage of the expected large number of telephone calls, the Plan negotiated a contract with a multiple employer trust to handle smaller group sales (2 to 25 employees) and beefed up its own sales force by hiring more telephone sales, group service, and news business representatives, besides opening offices in Goliath's territory.

Personal experience and research showed that television pulled the most responses at lowest cost per response, perhaps in part because the campaign was helped instead of being overwhelmed by Goliath's advertising. Many viewers did not differentiate between the two companies, but called the Roanoke-based one. Newspapers were next most effective, followed by radio.

At the end of the third quarter of the year—that is, the three months of the campaign—Blue Cross and Blue Shield of Southwestern Virginia had sold health care coverage to 587 new groups, more than four times the number sold in the same quarter of the previous year, and nearly seven times the sales of its five-times-larger competitor!

During the entire year of 1983, Blue Cross and Blue Shield of Southwestern Virginia enrolled 2036 new employer groups with about 40,000 employees—

a 50% increase in the number of groups enrolled over the previous year, making it number one out of more than 70 plans in the nation in this respect.

Even though 90% of the advertising appeared in June and July 1983, the effect on sales continued long after. In the first quarter of 1984, 1172 new groups, consisting of 38,000 subscribers, were added.

The importance of emphasizing the telephone number in direct response advertising cannot be overemphasized.

WHICH INVESTMENT ADVISORY AD PULLED BETTER?

On January 3, 1983, during a bull market, the two Standard & Poor's advertisements on the following pages each occupied four-fifths of a page in *Barron's Weekly* as part of an A–B split run. They sought subscriptions to Standard & Poor's Outlook, an investment advisory service which is distinctly different from Standard & Poor's factual research reports.

"The ads were designed basically to appeal to the needs of the more experienced, serious-minded investor," explains Dick Fernandes, Vice President and Account Supervisor at Doremus & Company, who directed the writing of the ads and guided the layouts. "Both were aimed at investors who would be more likely to remain a subscriber for an extended period of time, versus the 'shopper' or more fickle investor who regularly purchases short-term subscriptions to newsletters."

"The 'Wealth and Wisdom' ad was intended to appeal primarily to the more conservative investor, while the 'Our Trial Offer' ad was created to have a wider appeal," Fernandes said.

As you can see, both ads stimulate the desires of the investor. There was no brand differentiation, even though this is an intensive, competitive field. An estimated 3000 investment-type newsletters are published, of which about 300 actively advertise for subscriptions.

Both ads capitalized on Standard & Poor's extensive experience, longevity, and prestige; included the popular S&P *Encyclopedia* as a premium; and contained every possible stimulus for eliciting replies: coupon, toll-free number, choice of payment (check, credit card, billing), and of course, a money-back guarantee if not satisfied.

Respondents were given a choice of subscribing for 13 weeks for $29.95 or for one year for $175. The rationale given for taking a one-year subscription was "I don't want to risk interruption of service." One-year subscribers also received an S&P *Stock Guide* as a bonus, in addition to the encyclopedia.

In considering which ad pulled better, ask yourself not only which pulled more total dollars but which pulled more trials, which pulled more one-year subscriptions (if any), and which you would choose to place most often in the future. The answers to each question may (or may not) be different.

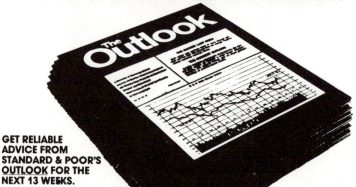

43

BOTH ADS WERE SMASHING SUCCESSES!

Investment advisory advertisers usually do not expect to make an immediate profit on their advertising. Because of the intensive competition, they usually expect to lose money on the advertising, but to make a profit over time by converting trial subscriptions into full-year subscriptions and, most of all, from renewals.

But these ads immediately pulled more than their space cost. The cost of the ads was $5706. The total amount received immediately was $6291. Here are the results:

	"Our Trial Offer"		"Wisdom and Wealth"	
	Number	Dollars Rec'd	Number	Dollars Rec'd
Trials	99	$2965	76	$2276
Year	2	350	4	700
	101	$3315	80	$2976

Neither the advertiser nor the agency was surprised that the "Our Trial Offer" ad pulled more replies, since it emphasized the trial offer in the headline and so would naturally draw more respondents interested in trial offers.

The response to the "Wisdom and Wealth" ad was more gratifying, even though the numbers of replies and the total dollars received were lower, because the respondents were thought more likely to become long-time subscribers.

"One of the problems in the industry," says Fernandes, "is that while there are about a million long-term subscribers to investment advisory publications, four or five times as many regularly take out trial subscriptions and never convert to yearly or longer subscriptions."

Further, the difference between the two ads was statistically slight in terms of dollars received.

In addition, it was felt that "Wisdom and Wealth" could stand repeating more often than "Our Trial Offer." "Wisdom and Wealth" built up The Outlook like an image advertisement. "Our Trial Offer" was obviously more opportunistic.

The advertiser and the agency therefore decided to place the "Wisdom and Wealth" ad most often and to spot the "Our Trial Offer" ad at times when "tax-deductible" would have the most appeal, such as before tax deadlines and at year end. By placing both ads in this way, it was felt that profits would be maximized.

3

VISIT-OUR-OFFICE FINANCIAL ADVERTISING

The principles for direct response advertising have been developed by counting coupons and telephone calls and noting which advertising characteristics result in the most returns and which in the least. However, many financial advertisers, particularly banks, want prospects to act in a different way. They want them to personally visit one of their offices.

Because of the difficulty of measuring, we don't have the same precise evidence for this kind of response that we have for coupon returns and telephone calls, but experience and logic indicate that the same principles apply, with three modifications. All three spring from the difficulty of getting people to go to the financial organization's place of business. Causing people to walk, drive, or otherwise travel is harder to accomplish than getting them to clip a coupon or make a telephone call.

Consequently, (1) more money may need to be budgeted to get the same number of people to act, (2) the benefit may need to be even stronger than for a coupon or telephone response, and (3) memorability is necessary. Prospects can't be expected to immediately leave their TV sets or put down their newspapers to go to the bank or other place of business. In fact, the offices are probably closed when most prospects are watching or reading. But if they remember the benefit and where they can get it, they will go to the bank or investment firm or insurance agency when it's convenient for them—perhaps the next day, perhaps on their way to work or at lunchtime, perhaps when they're in the neighborhood.

Repetition of the advertisement or commercial can make the benefit and the advertiser memorable, but the best visit-our-office advertisements and commercials don't depend upon repetition alone for memorability. The advertisement or commercial itself combines memorability with a strong benefit. Some examples are shown in the case histories on the following pages.

In one case history, the anguish of a man hammering on the door of a closed bank made the advantages of an automatic teller machine ATM memorable. In the second case history, boldly stating the name of a competing bank made the dollar amount that could be saved on a loan stick in the minds of readers and listeners.

An advertisement that Howard Zieff, a great photographer, and I created while I was at Doremus & Company, made the true benefits of a home improvement loan deeply felt and therefore remembered and acted upon, even though it appeared only once in each of three New York City newspapers.

Some questioning had revealed several facts, the most important of which were: (1) Most home improvement loans were for installing an up-to-date kitchen. (2) Most of the loans were obtained by the husband. Consequently, the advertisement aimed at causing husbands to take out home improvement loans for their wives' sakes. It featured a large, memorable photograph of a modern kitchen with a man in his early thirties receiving a big, affectionate kiss from his wife. The headline was "Give her the kitchen she deserves with a Chemical home improvement loan."

Visit-our-office advertisements and commercials may appear to be image advertising to the uninitiated, but the successful ones follow direct response rules, with memorability added.

NEGATIVE BENEFITS STIMULATE USAGE OF ATMs

The Connecticut Bank and Trust Company, the largest bank in Connecticut, had installed automatic teller machines, nicknamed "Barneys," in front of 39 offices. But the Barneys weren't being used much. Five years after their installation only 60,000 people held cards. Transactions per machine averaged only 1800 per month.

In 1978 an advertising campaign was launched with the objective of doubling ATM usage. Television and radio commercials, newspaper ads, and collateral material were created by the advertising agency, Mintz & Hoke Inc., and placed directly by the bank, under the direction of the bank's advertising manager, Bill Large.

The TV commercials were placed on network-affiliated stations, one in Hartford and two in New Haven. Combined, they blanketed the state. Programs were chosen to catch viewing by those who research showed were most likely to use ATMs, the "early adapters"—early and late news, "60 Minutes," weekend football, "Good Morning America," and "General Hospital."

Each commercial or ad aroused the emotions of viewers and listeners by dramatizing the frustration of waiting in line or of needing money when the bank is closed.

Connecticut Bank and Trust Co. TV Commercial (30 seconds)

Video	Audio
MAN HAMMERING ON DOOR OF BANK:	ANNCR: Ever notice when you need cash the most, banks seem to be open the least?
MS WOMAN USING BARNEY:	Well, CBT's changing all that . . . with Barney. Barney is like having a teller on duty 24 hours a day.
CU HAND GETTING CASH FROM BARNEY:	With Barney, you can make deposits, pay loans, check your account balances . . . even get cash any time you need it.
CU WOMAN FACING CAMERA:	WOMAN: Is there anything Barney won't do?
MS BARNEY SHOWING LOGO:	ANNCR: Sure . . . close. CBT. The bank that never closes.

During the first eight months of the campaign, about $250,000 was spent, mostly on television. Card sales climbed from a rate of 4200 per month to 9500. Use of ATMs increased even faster. Transactions per machine per month went from 1800 to 4000 in just six weeks! As the advertising continued, the number of cardholders and the usage increased further. By 1984 more than 270,000 peopled owned Barney cards.

COMPARATIVE ADVERTISING BOOSTS LOAN VOLUME

California First Bank decided to increase its consumer loan volume by $30 million in a few weeks. The bank could lend money for the purchase of an automobile or other big-ticket item at a lower interest rate than its larger competitors, such as Bank of America, but was much less well known. Its image advertising had been sporadic at best.

To be successful, therefore, the advertising needed to do more than just to make consumers *aware* that they could borrow money at lower cost from California First. Consumers had to be made to *feel* the difference very strongly. The reluctance of many to deal with a bank they had never, or only vaguely, heard of had to be overcome. Furthermore, consumers had to be motivated so strongly that they would go to the trouble of finding out where the nearest California First branch was, visit it in person, and go through the process of taking out a loan. Financing is much easier through the dealer from whom one buys a car, boat, motor home, etc.; borrowing much easier from a bank through which one already has a relationship.

The solution was advertising that converted the difference in interest rates into savings in dollars. (A technique used in the discount brokerage ad at the end of Chapter One.)

Each headline drew a direct money comparison with a competing bank, naming the competitor. For example: **This motor home costs $2,186 more at First Interstate.** Naming the bank was even more effective if the reader already had a relationship with the named bank, but it was also effective with other readers because the named banks were so well known.

The attention of readers was gained through the use of dominating photographs of big ticket items that a consumer might borrow money to buy. A person about to buy an automobile will carefully scrutinize automobile ads, someone about to buy a boat will examine boat ads, etc. And these items have such general interest that many other potential borrowers would peruse them as well, concluding that they also might be able to save money at California First.

The inherent advantages of print were utilized well. A table of specific figures, showing how the dollar savings were arrived at, convinced readers that the savings were not just advertising puffery. And an important second benefit was included in the copy—a quick answer to a loan application.

A Comparison	California First	Security Pacific
Annual Percentage Rate on $13,840	13.5%	15%
Monthly Payments	$ 374.72	385.15
x 48 Months	$ 17,986.56	18,487.20
$ Difference	$	+ 500.64

Rates determined by independent survey taken October 12, 1983.

THIS CAR COSTS $500 MORE AT SECURITY PACIFIC.

It's true.

A loan for this 1984 Ford Thunderbird Turbo will cost you $500 more at Security Pacific, than it will at California First.

The fact is, California First Bank has the lowest fixed rates on consumer loans, *overall*, of any major bank in the state. So no matter what you need the money for, California First could wind up saving you more than you think.

In addition, if the loan you want is under $50,000, and isn't secured by real estate, we'll answer your request within 24 hours. Sometimes the same day.

We think lower rates on loans, and faster answers, are two good ways to show how much better a bank we can be.

If you'd like to know *how much* better, think of how much farther you could go on $500.

CALIFORNIA FIRST BANK

Member FDIC

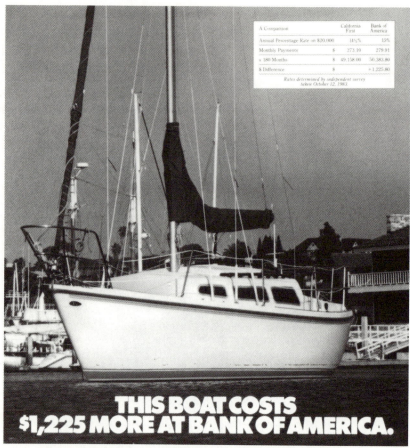

A Comparison		California First	Bank of America
Annual Percentage Rate on $20,000		14½%	15%
Monthly Payments	$	273.10	279.91
x 180 Months	$	49,158.00	50,383.80
$ Difference	$		+1,225.80

Rates determined by independent survey taken October 12, 1983.

THIS BOAT COSTS
$1,225 MORE AT BANK OF AMERICA.

It's true.

A loan for this Catalina 27 sailboat will cost you $1,225 more at Bank of America, than it will at California First.

The fact is, California First Bank has the lowest fixed rates on consumer loans, *overall*, of any major bank in the state. So no matter what you need the money for, California First could wind up saving you more than you think.

In addition, if the loan you want is under $50,000, and isn't secured by real estate, we'll answer your request within 24 hours. Sometimes the same day.

We think lower rates on loans, and faster answers, are two good ways to prove how much better banking can be at California First.

If you'd like to know *how much* better, think of how much more you'd enjoy a new boat with $1,225 in your pocket.

CALIFORNIA FIRST BANK
Member FDIC

Consumers usually want to complete their purchases as soon as possible and may be in the middle of arranging financing another way when they see the ad.

For three weeks, the advertisements appeared twice weekly in the *Los Angeles Times* and the *San Diego Tribune*, once weekly in the *San Francisco Chronicle/Examiner*, and once or twice weekly in local newspapers.

Radio supplemented the newspaper advertising in order to increase awareness and add excitement, as well as for the synergism that results from the use of more than one medium. Sound effects stimulated listening and related the savings to specific purchases. One-hundred-and-twenty-five gross rating points spread over three weeks were bought on Los Angeles stations; 100 gross rating points on San Francisco stations were spread over three weeks.

There was not enough time to produce a television commercial. Anyway, the budget was too small—less than $500,000.

In four weeks, the bank opened 1400 new loan accounts, lending $40 million, 30% more than the marketing goal. The advertising obviously also made California First better known and helped it gain the reputation of being a low-cost lender. The agency was Ogilvy & Mather—San Francisco.

California First Bank Radio Commercial (one minute)

SFX:	CAR ENGINE REVVING
ANNCR:	A Ford Thunderbird Turbo costs $500 more at Security Pacific.
SFX:	SAILBOAT SOUNDS
ANNCR:	A Catalina 27 sailboat costs $1,225 more at Bank of America.
SFX:	HAMMER, POWER SAW
ANNCR:	And a room addition on an average house costs $3,202 more at Wells Fargo.
	(SFX FADE OUT) Based on the same repayment period, that's how much more a loan would cost at those other banks, when compared to California First.
	You see, California First has the lowest fixed loan rates, *overall*, of any major bank in the state.
	So whether you're thinking about a loan for a new camper...
SFX:	OWL HOOTING
ANNCR:	...a swimming pool...
SFX:	DIVE INTO POOL
ANNCR:	...a motorboat...
SFX:	BOAT ENGINE CHURNING
ANNCR:	...or even a European holiday...
SFX:	SHIP HORN BLOWING
ANNCR:	...check into California First. The savings could add up to more than you think...
SFX:	ADDING MACHINE
2nd ANNCR:	California First Bank. An equal housing lender. Member FDIC.

4

FINANCIAL IMAGE AND REMINDER ADVERTISING

The reputation of a marketer of financial services counts for much more than in other industries. People will sometimes buy a product from somebody they don't know, even from a street vendor, but most people always look for a financial organization they can trust. For several reasons, they instinctively avoid any organization in which they lack confidence. First, the amount of money involved is usually substantial—hundreds, thousands, even millions of dollars. Second, the customer usually depends upon the financial organization for some advice, much of which the customer either cannot check or does not have the time or will to check. Third, most benefits are not received immediately. Interest and dividends are paid over an extensive period of time—capital gains at some indeterminate future date, accident insurance when an accident occurs, life insurance after death.

Consequently, banks, investment firms, and insurance companies have long engaged in advertising that aims to improve the way they are regarded, besides making them favorably known to a larger number of possible customers.

Historically, financial marketers have used image advertising mostly to quiet fears. After the numerous bank failures of the 1930s, bank advertising emphasized financial strength, even though most deposits were insured by the federal government.

As the years went by and bank failures faded in the minds of older people and became only history to younger prospects, bank marketers changed the central theme of their image advertising to quieting a different fear—that of being turned down for a loan. A typical slogan of the period was "You've got a friend at Bankers Trust." The "friend" theme was a reaction to the strength-emphasizing advertising, which many marketers felt intimidated possible customers, especially younger people. It also resulted from a shift in the primary needs of most banks—for loans rather than for deposits.

In the investment business, modern advertising also began by quieting fears. And it too resulted from a need that originated internally, in this instance within one investment firm, Merrill Lynch. In the decade following World War II, the survival, not merely the profitability, of Merrill Lynch depended upon the success of its image advertising.

We'll examine the Merrill Lynch advertising of the post–World War II decades not only for its historical interest but for other reasons as well. We'll see how a highly successful image campaign evolved. The examination will also serve as a means of contrasting the principles of image, direct response, and reminder advertising—principles that apply not only to investment advertising but also to bank and insurance advertising.

Merrill Lynch, Pierce, Fenner & Beane was formed just prior to World War II by the merger of several firms, the largest of which was E. A. Pierce & Co. During the 1930s, E. A. Pierce & Co. had become the nation's largest brokerage firm. However, it had become the largest in an unhealthy way. As firm after firm approached failure following the 1929 stock market crash, officials of the New York Stock Exchange urged many firms nearing failure to merge with E. A. Pierce & Co. Consequently, as E. A. Pierce became larger it also became weaker.

Charles E. Merrill instituted a number of reforms that not only strengthened "The Thundering Herd" internally, but also initiated a new kind of advertising that contrasted sharply with the advertising of other investment firms.

Most investment advertising of the post–World War II period consisted of tombstones—that is, announcements of new issues or just the name of the firm with a simple statement of its business. (Advertisements announcing offerings of new issues of securities are nick-named "tombstones" because each ad consists largely of the listing of the names of the underwriters, just like gravestones—and perhaps also because the ads are generally so mournful looking. The term is often stretched to include other financial ads.)

A few, but growing number of firms, such as E. F. Hutton, placed advertisements that aimed at obtaining leads for their salesmen. (There were few if any female brokers in those days.) The ads usually offered a free research report or other booklet. The best of these had a headline featuring the benefit the reader could expect, a small illustration of the booklet, copy that was as hard-sell as the New York Stock Exchange would allow (which was not very hard), and a coupon.

The advertisement that long held the record of the number of inquiries received from an ad in *The New York Times*, for Reynolds & Co., is shown on the opposite page. It may still hold the record for cost-per-response (21¢), partly because of inflation.

This ad differs from other direct response advertisements in that the ad was written first and the booklet written afterward to meet the description in the ad. Note that the ad was written so as to appeal to virtually every investor, and it

(Slightly reduced in size)

used virtually every possible direct response technique. The processing of the responses also differed. Instead of handing the coupons to account executives, they were followed up by a direct mail letter, and the names of investors responding to the mailing were given to account executives.

The headlines of Hutton, Reynolds, and other direct response advertisers needed to be specific and hard-hitting if the ads were to draw inquiries in large quantities. They needed to cause investors to act at the time they were thinking of buying stocks—to make themselves known as hot prospects.

The Merrill Lynch advertisements were entirely different. The headlines usually attempted to arouse the curiosity of the reader, the tone was quietly informative, and there was seldom a coupon to clip. Sometimes, but not always, the ad suggested that the reader visit a Merrill Lynch office.

The headlines and copy had to be such that they would attract readership from investors and potential investors at times when they were not thinking of investing. So the headlines were broad, not selective. The creative challenge was to attract readers when they were not thinking about investing.

Merrill Lynch's advertising aimed to counter the nervousness many people felt about investing in stocks, which had been aroused by the loose practices of the 1920s and the serious losses many investors suffered in the 1930s. The advertising could not aim solely or even primarily at attracting customers away from other firms if Merrill Lynch were to survive. People who had been soured on common stocks needed to be attracted back into the market, and people who had never bought stocks before had to be attracted into the stock market for the first time.

Early Merrill Lynch advertising centered around two themes. One was "The customers' interest comes first." The advertising told how "customers' men" had been renamed "account executives" to emphasize the different attitude they had at Merrill Lynch. "Account executive" was a term borrowed from the advertising industry, where the conflict of interest is similar. An advertising account executive is supposed to give customers advice that may run counter to his or her own pecuniary advantage (and many do). The more the advertiser spends, the more money the agency realizes. Bigger ads are more profitable than smaller ones, because the agency's costs are nearly the same, regardless of an ad's size.

Similarly, in investing, the more a customer invests and the more often he buys and sells, the more money the investment firm makes. And if the account executive shares in the commissions—as was the rule then and is the rule today—it is in his or her own interest to encourage frequent trading.

To counter this fear that customers' accounts would be churned, Merrill Lynch account executives were paid a salary, beginning in the 1940s, and this fact was trumpeted time and time again in the advertising.

The other principal theme of Merrill Lynch advertising countered the fear that potential investors would be hoodwinked by not being told all they needed to know. The slogan was "Investigate before you invest."

What should everybody do with their extra money?

Invest it in good common stocks.

Why?

Because we think it has a chance to grow with the years —a good chance.

Because most common stocks in sound, well-managed companies pay dividends to their stockholders most years.

Then why do we insist on saying your "extra money?" Because anybody who buys stock takes the risk that he might be forced to sell it sometime in the future for less than he paid for it.

Stock prices do go down as well as up. They always have, they always will.

The chart on any recognized index of stock prices consists of peaks and valleys. But peaks and valleys notwithstanding, ever since the turn of the century, that same chart will show an upward trend of about 3% a year.

Of course nobody can invest in all stocks—or an average stock either for that matter.

That's why careful selection of the stocks that seem appropriate to your particular purposes at any particular time will always be of primary importance in any successful investment program.

And in that selection—for any sum, or any objective— we don't know of anybody in our business more ready, or willing, or able, to help.

MERRILL LYNCH, PIERCE, FENNER & SMITH INC

MEMBERS NEW YORK STOCK EXCHANGE AND OTHER PRINCIPAL STOCK AND COMMODITY EXCHANGES

70 Pine Street, New York 5—Whitehall 4-1212

575 Madison Ave., N.Y. 22	MU 8-6161	333 Seventh Ave., N.Y. 1	LW 4-1255
Time-Life Bldg., N.Y. 20	JU 2-1313	Brooklyn: 200 Montague St.	UL 8-6400
61 W. 48th St., N.Y. 20	CI 6-4500	Brooklyn: 2231 Church Ave.	UL 6-6242
1451 Broadway, N.Y. 36	LO 3-6474	Forest Hills: 70-49 Austin St.	BO 1-4800
295 Madison Ave., N.Y. 17	MU 6-6767	Garden City: 1001 Franklin Ave.	CH 8-7000
500 Seventh Ave., N.Y. 18	LO 4-9200	Newark: 570 Broad St.	624-8600
320 Park Ave., N.Y. 22	PL 2-7200	Paramus: East 328 Route 4	DI 3-5747
Pan Am Bldg., N.Y. 17	TN 7-4040	Stamford: 80 W. Park Place	348-3781

Even as late as 1964, when this ad appeared (actual size) in *The New York Times*, Merrill Lynch advertising aimed at turning non-investors into investors.

Early Merrill Lynch advertising also differed from that of other investment firms in its continuity. For investors and potential investors to be convinced that the firm's policies were new and unique, they needed to read about the firm repeatedly. Attitudes are seldom changed with a single telling. So advertisements were placed weekly in the financial pages of *The New York Times* and newspapers in other cities where Merrill Lynch had offices.

Few full-page—or even quarter-page—ads were placed in the 1940s, 1950s, and 1960s, either by Merrill Lynch or by its competitors. Competitors did not place large space ads because smaller ads pull responses more efficiently. A full-page ad, for example, will seldom, if ever, pull twice the responses of a half-page ad, a half-page ad will seldom pull twice the responses of a quarter-page ad. And an eighth of a page is usually more cost-effective than a quarter page.

This ad appeared in *The New York Times* on Wednesday, November 24, 1948.

"Chance of a Lifetime!"

That's the kind of advice you *won't* get from Merrill Lynch. "Flyers" to us are still boys with wings.

But if you're interested in sound investments in securities — our services might help.

We supply basic facts — both favorable *and* unfavorable — about any stock or company.

Want to see samples? Write or call for our latest "Security and Industry Survey" — There's no charge.

Department A-40

MERRILL LYNCH, PIERCE, FENNER & BEANE
Underwriters and Distributors of Investment Securities
Brokers in Securities and Commodities

70 PINE STREET, NEW YORK 5, N. Y.
Telephone: WHitehall 4-1212

Uptown Office: *Newark:*
730 FIFTH AVE. (at 57th St.)   744 BROAD STREET
Tel. CIrcle 7-0900   Tel. MArket 3-8300

Stamford—80 West Park Place—Tel: 4-1171

This ad appeared (actual size) in *The New York Times* on Wednesday, November 17, 1948.

Returns from direct response advertisements have been collected and correlated with the size of the ad. For smaller ads, as the size increases, the returns increase proportionately, but as the ads become larger, the returns increase less than proportionately. In an optimum direct response ad, every additional inch of space, every line, every word increases the number of respondents in proportion to the cost of the additional space, line, or word.

But Merrill Lynch's advertising did not aim at attracting responses but at changing attitudes. And larger advertisements have a unique impact on readers, independent of their content. Large ads cause readers to feel that the advertiser is big and strong. Surveys show that readers tend to equate the size of the ad with the size of the company. It's conspicuous consumption in advertising. Only large, strong firms can afford big ads, readers feel. And it's not illogical.

Since most people—and especially most investors—prefer to do business with big, strong companies, why didn't Merrill Lynch place only dominating-size advertisements? Why did it for many years regularly place ads that were the same size as those of its competitors?

The most successful image campaigns, such as the historic Avis "We try harder" advertising, consist of ads of dominating size placed with frequency close enough to build up a lasting impression. In image advertising, as in package goods advertising, memorability is important. An image must reach and influence people not only when they are ready to buy, but long before.

Since all advertising budgets are limited to some extent, image campaigns are usually placed in flights, say, once a week for a couple of months, then a hiatus, then another flight.

Merrill Lynch did not follow this policy. Instead, it placed mostly small plus a few large advertisements such as a historic full-page ad with the headline "What Every Investor Should Know About This Stock and Bond Business." Merrill Lynch ran small ads every week in the year because the advertising needed to perform another function besides communicating the firm's distinctive nature and size. Investors needed to be reminded of Merrill Lynch's existence and the location of the nearest office at the time they were interested in buying or selling stocks. Both new and old customers needed to know the location of the nearest Merrill Lynch office because of a cost-saving measure taken by Charlie Merrill to save the firm. He had moved many offices of the newly merged firm out of ground-floor locations to upper floors, where the rents were considerably cheaper. Consequently, investors needed to be told where to go to get all the wonderful benefits Merrill Lynch was offering. Merrill Lynch needed to be in newspapers every week, and large space advertisements every week would have been prohibitively costly.

It was not until the 1970s, when many Merrill Lynch offices had returned to ground-floor locations, and in any case were too numerous to list in ads, that the offices were not named—and only large image advertisements were placed.

In other words, early Merrill Lynch ads were reminder advertising as well as image advertising.

While similar to image advertising, the principles of *reminder advertising* are slightly different. Reminder advertising is done by businesses that provide services that customers need only occasionally, such as restaurants, funeral homes, tourist attractions, and consultants of various kinds. Reminder advertising tells potential customers that the business exists and gives them the address of the business. The ads may contain a benefit and may make some attempt to communicate a distinctive image, but the ads principally tell potential customers "This is what we do and here is where we are."

Reminder advertisements usually appear weekly in the appropriate publications and are small. They must appear weekly so that potential customers will not be lost. Potential customers need to see the ad and know that the business exists at the time they need the service. The ads can be small because potential cus-

(Actual size)

tomers usually look for them. Attracting attention through large size is not necessary. And the need to appear weekly makes it too costly for the ads to be large.

Consequently, Merrill Lynch advertisements were mostly of modest size and appeared weekly in local newspapers to serve as reminders while at the same time they communicated a distinctive image.

Merrill Lynch ads also differed from most image campaigns outside the financial industry in that they were usually all-type. They were all-type not only because of the inherent difficulty of illustrating any financial advertising, as previously discussed, but also because of the particular difficulty in illustrating the new principles under which Merrill Lynch was operating. Words could perform that function better than pictures in the space that the budget and other considerations allowed for each ad.

Generally speaking, an illustration, so long as it is pertinent, usually improves the results aimed at by any advertisement. But large illustrations are not usually cost-effective for direct response ads because the additional space does not usually increase the number of responses proportionate to the cost of the increased space. However, a small, functional illustration can increase responses more than additional words.

When the purpose of the advertising is to arouse an emotion favorable to the advertiser and to cause readers to remember the ad and the advertiser, a large, dominating illustration can be very effective. In most non-financial image ads, the photography or other illustration takes up more space than the copy and the signature. And rightly so.

In the 1950s, Paine, Webber, Jackson & Curtis began a campaign which, even though small space, took advantage of the attention-getting power of illustrations. Paine, Webber, Jackson & Curtis, like Merrill Lynch, knew that its advertisements needed to appear weekly in local newspapers to remind people who were ready to invest that the firm existed and where the nearest office was. But Paine, Webber, Jackson & Curtis did not have the distinctive character that Merrill Lynch had. It was less than half the size, its account executives were on commission, and the volume of its research publications was modest compared to Merrill Lynch's cornucopia.

The image-reminder advertisements of Paine, Webber, Jackson & Curtis therefore did not attempt to communicate any distinctive features of the firm, but simply concentrated on investors' needs and fears—made investors aware that they could get certain benefits by becoming customers of the firm. And since nobody else was doing this kind of advertising at the time, a distinctive image was communicated by default.

Paine, Webber, Jackson & Curtis also placed direct response advertisements in order to gain leads for its account executives. Because enough leads could be obtained by placing direct response ads every other week, the direct response ads were alternated with image ads, both serving as reminder ads.

(Actual size)

The direct response advertisements followed direct response copy principles, and the image ads followed image ad copy principles—which were being applied to financial advertising for the first time.

For several reasons, the Merrill Lynch and Paine, Webber, Jackson & Curtis ads seem mild compared to the image advertising of today. (1) The copy did not need to make them better than other investment firms. Just their placing image advertising did that. Their main competitors in those days were banks and insurance companies. The copy aimed to cause people to put some of their money into stocks instead of all into savings accounts and insurance. (2) To say this more strongly would have been counterproductive because of the fearful attitude toward brokerage firms in those days. (3) The New York Stock Exchange would not have allowed such advertising.

The Merrill Lynch advertisements of the 1950s and 1960s were written mostly by Jack Adams, a Navy pilot who joined Merrill Lynch's then agency, Albert Frank–Guenther Law, immediately after World War II. A few ads were written by Merrill Lynch's advertising manager, Louis Engel, who had previously been editor of *BusinessWeek*.

Two former Merrill Lynchers were involved in the Paine, Webber ads. J. Luttrell "Whitey" Maclin had been a star reporter on *The Herald Tribune* before World War II, a glider pilot during the war, and then public relations director at Merrill Lynch. He was recruited by Paine, Webber, Jackson & Curtis in 1952 to modernize their advertising and public relations. I, who had been a public relations and promotion writer under Whitey at Merrill Lynch and had left to collaborate on a couple of books, joined Doremus & Company in 1953 as a copywriter, working on the Paine, Webber, Jackson & Curtis, Hutton, Reynolds, and other accounts. Barry McMenniman, later president of Doremus, and Frank Schaffer, later Doremus chairman, were the principal account executives.

Our examination of the early advertising of Merrill Lynch and its competition has illustrated many of the differences between image advertising and direct response advertising. But what about white space and the general appearance of the advertisement? And what about color? Type size?

White space, tastefully used, can improve the image of the advertiser, but it does not increase responses proportionate to the additional cost, if it does so at all. White space doesn't sell because it does little toward compelling readers to act. Skillfully used, however, white space can make an advertisement more pleasing and tasteful, and therefore cause some readers to want to be associated with such a bank or company, but the feeling aroused is comparatively weak. Surveys show that a lower cost per response can usually be obtained either by making the ad smaller or by using the additional space for selling copy.

The case is similar for color. Full color can make an advertisement more attractive and gain greater attention. But financial ads with some color or full color don't draw responses or memorability proportional to their additional cost.

The same is true for type size. Direct response ads can have very small type—

8-point, 7-point, even 6-point, if the headline is strong enough. But small type is harder to read especially by the tired eyes of older people—and older people have the most money. So image advertisements must have type that's 9- or 10-point or larger.

Advertisers are sometimes tempted to place a coupon in an image advertisement. Doing so will result in some responses, but surveys show that a coupon usually reduces the readership of the ad. The probable reason: the coupon detracts from the mood of the image ad. It is emotionally jarring. A coupon does not contribute to the intent of an image ad, which is to change attitude.

A comparison of the principles of direct response advertising and image advertising in the print media follows. To see the principles successfully applied, see the CIGNA case history in Chapter 1 and the Morgan Guaranty case history at the end of this chapter.

How the Principles of Direct Response and Image Advertising in the Print Media Compare

	Direct Response	Image
Objective	Immediate action	Improved attitude
Headline	Benefit	Flexible
Size	No bigger than necessary	Dominating desirable
Repetition	Not necessary	Usually necessary
Illustration	Functional, usually small	Emotional, usually large
Coupon	Increases returns	Decreases readership
White space	Doesn't increase number of responses	Can enhance image
Small type size	OK	No good
Color	Seldom cost-effective	Can enhance image
Size of logo	Small	Large

USING THE SAME EFFECTIVE FORMAT YEAR AFTER YEAR, A WHOLESALE BANK GAINS HIGH RECOGNITION OF DESIRABLE QUALITIES

Major competitors of The Morgan Bank regularly spend millions more dollars on advertising their wholesale banking services than Morgan does. These competitors also spend additional millions advertising retail services, which Morgan doesn't provide.

Yet objective surveys consistently show that financial officers of large companies remember Morgan's advertising on an unaided basis better than the corporate advertising of all its bigger-spending competitors except one. That competitor regularly spends more than twice as much advertising its wholesale services as does Morgan. But it gains top-of-the-mind awareness only a shade higher than Morgan, making Morgan's recall-per-dollar-spent much higher.

So far as favorable impressions are concerned, Morgan's advertising outscores every one of its bigger-spending competitors by a wide margin. For example, one nationwide survey showed that many more financial officers said Morgan's advertising was most believable, communicated best, and contained the most useful information. Further, when asked how well each bank's advertising reflected the true nature of the bank, four times as many ranked Morgan's advertising at the top as they did the next highest bank. Similar research among financial officers of large institutions in both Europe and Asia have produced similar results.

Another in-depth survey showed that The Morgan Bank's advertising impressed financial officers of Fortune 500 companies more favorably than the advertising of any other bank. And the larger the company, the greater the likelihood that the financial officer was most impressed by Morgan's advertising.

The Wall Street Journal gets more of Morgan's annual budget of a few million dollars than any other medium. Bruce Roberts, Advertising Vice President of The Morgan Bank, says, "We place full-page advertisements so frequently in The Wall Street Journal, including its overseas editions, because 99% of U.S. financial officers in our market read it carefully every day." Morgan's advertising also appears in Fortune, Forbes, BusinessWeek, The Financial Times, The Economist, business and financial media around the world, and trade publications—nearly 100 publications in all. Many of the bank's ads are adapted to local languages, a total of 13.

The advertising follows the well-established format for effective image advertising. A large, dominating rectangular halftone, featuring Morgan people with their names and specialties in a caption, gains attention and sparks memorability. A headline, set in initial capital and lower case for easy comprehension, always contains "Morgan" or "The Morgan Bank," thus securely tying the bank to the benefit. The advertising is effective even if the reader goes no further. Big type makes the copy attractive to read, even for those who are only mildly interested. The signature does not use the formal name for the bank (Morgan Guaranty Trust Company) but the easier-to-remember The Morgan Bank. It is set in type smaller than the headline in the interests of good taste and to communicate the feeling that Morgan places the benefit to customers first.

Within this format, creative people concentrate on relating the service

How Morgan works to make your cash management the best in the business

On a tour of the bank's operations facilities, two Morgan officers–cash management specialist Leonard Penn and account manager Gary Herbst, standing at right–show global communications control console to a client.

The best cash management answers your company's needs precisely—this day, this hour.

And your needs change as fast as markets and financing demands and opportunities change.

Meeting these needs is critical to the multinational market The Morgan Bank serves, where large-dollar transactions are at stake and our attention to detail makes the difference.

That's why we hone our cash management services continuously—to make them more adaptable, more timely, more useful, more responsive—to be the best in the business in terms of your company's specific needs. Here's how we serve major corporations like yours.

Morgan innovates with technology. Morgan is well known for cash management ideas. But newness isn't our only measure of worth. Every new service or system must add value, produce a measurable client benefit, be flexible enough to respond to change.

One example is MORCOM, Morgan's computerized communications system. Among the first to be fully automated, it delivers on-line money transfer information in seconds and allows you to input your

instructions with maximum security.

Another is our controlled disbursement facility at Morgan Bank (Delaware). It gives you each day's checks-paid total on your terminal early enough so you can make timely and profitable borrowing and investment decisions.

We've also been a pioneer over the years. Morgan developed the first electronic cash letter service for correspondent banks. We were the first to offer centralized depository transfer checks, the first with a balance reporting system accessible worldwide by terminal.

Morgan advises on developments. We make it our business to keep up with significant cash management developments, and to communicate them to you clearly. We're up-to-the-minute on everything from ACH to treasury workstations. We help you understand and evaluate new technologies, new regulations—to show how they could affect your cash management systems and plans.

Morgan pairs speed with accuracy. Speed is crucial in cash management, but not at the expense of accuracy. Tracking down and correcting errors

costs time and money. That's why we give accuracy, dependability, and speed equal importance. No wonder leading financial surveys rank Morgan's operations services tops in thoroughness and reliability as well as timeliness.

To be more responsive, Morgan adapts. Morgan's customer service specialists, who know our systems and your needs, provide fast, focused responses to your questions. They monitor your transactions closely to anticipate problems. And our computerized investigations tracking system instantly tells you the status of all your money transfer inquiries.

Since no company has identical needs, cash management solutions at Morgan are flexible. Our systems are both modular and interactive, so we can assemble just the combination of services that's right for you.

An invitation to see our systems. We'd like to show you why so many financial officers now use Morgan for cash management. Ask the Morgan banker who calls on you to set up an appointment to see our systems at work. Or write or call Michel Tilmant, Vice President, Operations Services, Morgan Guaranty Trust Company, 23 Wall Street, New York, NY 10015. Telephone (212) 483-2785. Member FDIC

The Morgan Bank

being advertised as informatively and clearly as possible to the target audience. Claims are backed up with evidence.

While talented people involved in Morgan advertising have come and gone, three have been especially instrumental in establishing and maintaining this highly successful format for 15 years. They are Bruce Roberts at Morgan and Bruce Friedlich, President, and Robert H. Nutt, Senior Vice President, at the bank's international agency, Doyle Graf Mabley.

5

MORE ABOUT IMPROVING ATTITUDES AND INCREASING AWARENESS

Many of the principles of image advertising sound like the principles for advertising package goods but in practice the creator of image advertisements has much greater flexibility, must appeal to a much broader audience, has a wider, perhaps limitless, choice of ways to structure the ad or commercial, and usually cannot employ the hard-sell tone that often works for package goods advertising.

Both image advertising and package goods advertising require memorability. This is important in image advertising because a principal purpose is to pave the way for a sales call or to influence prospects before they are willing to buy. But the memorability in image advertising usually needs to be of a different sort. Instead of the conscious remembering necessary in package goods, the remembering may need to be a feeling toward the advertiser. The tone of the advertisement may be its most important attribute—as in the first of the nationwide image television commercials that follow.

Humor can be effective in image advertising because it will be remembered by many people who are not very interested in the advertiser at the time, but the humor must enhance the stature of the advertiser and not offend prospects—as shown by the second of the Nationwide image commercials that follow.

The need for memorability affects not only the form and content of the advertising, but also the frequency. Image advertising aims to change attitude. Repetition increases not only memorability but also believability. Cynics say, "Repeat anything often enough and everybody'll believe it."

Because an image advertisement must appeal to audiences other than those ready to buy, the headline and illustration need to have a much broader appeal than the beginning of a package goods commercial or ad.

In a true image advertisement, the final words reiterate the sense of the headline, perhaps more strongly, but other endings can be effective. An image ad may follow the outline of a newspaper story and just end with the least important information, or the last paragraph may suggest a telephone call. And while a good-sized logo is usually best, taste and other considerations may make it advisable to keep the logo modest-sized.

On television, successful financial image advertising follows principles similar to those for print advertising. The TV copywriter's main task is to hold the interest of as many viewers as possible, not just those ready to buy, as in a direct response or package goods advertisement. In fact, the copywriter has greater flexibility throughout because the purpose is to change attitudes, which can be done in many ways.

An image commercial may be structured in the here's-the-benefit-and-here's-how-to-get-it mode of direct response and package goods commercials, but usually it must be done subtly. Other structures, such as those of poetry or of the short story, usually are to be preferred.

Thirty seconds is usually adequate for an image TV commercial, but greater length can be useful. Creating a mood may require longer than 30 seconds, as the following TV image commercials show.

LOVE SELLS LIFE INSURANCE

Every year since 1969, Nationwide Insurance Company has spent millions of dollars a year to air commercials featuring love and life insurance. Often the commercials featured the love between a father and a son. After all, for many men their son's security and future—that the son will continue on after the father is dead—counts more than anything else. In these commercials, sometimes the father talks to the viewer, sometimes to the announcer, sometimes to the son; sometimes the voices are mixed.

The slogan "Nationwide is on your side" was not changed over all the years, and each commercial showed why the slogan is true.

The commercials thus promised a psychological benefit to the father while he was still alive—in effect promised him immortality. The commercials also made fathers feel that Nationwide was a company that could help them, while stimulating the morale of Nationwide's 4500 life insurance agents.

During the first 10 years in which these commercials appeared, sales of Nationwide life insurance increased 70% faster than in the industry as a whole, even though the number of Nationwide's insurance agents stayed about the same. The agency is Ogilvy & Mather Advertising.

1. (MUSIC UNDER) DAD: You ready? SON: Yeah. DAD: You sure? Okay.

2. hoist it up. Clean it off. SON: Okay Dad.

3. ANNCR: (VO) He's in your care so little time.

4. So you give him what you can.

5. Blue skies and laughter.

6. Freedom just to be a kid a little while.

7. DAD: Get ready to come about.

8. (VOICES UNDER) ANNCR: (VO) And you protect him until he learns from you how to protect himself.

9. At Nationwide we're part of that protection.

10. With Family Life Insurance Plans to cover every member of your family.

11. ANNCR: (VO) Now and in the future.

12. DAD: Pull on that line. ANNCR: (VO) To help you make sure he's taken care of.

13. DAD: Okay John, take over. ANNCR: (VO) Until he can take care of himself.

14. DAD: You got it? SON: I got it, Dad.

15. DAD: You're doing Okay. ANNCR: (VO) Family Life Insurance,

16. (SFX: LAUGHTER) part of Nationwide's blanket protection for you and your family.

17. CHORUS: You know who to count on for blanket protection

18. and know that you'll find peace of mind.

19. When Nationwide...Nationwide is on your side... on your side,

20. Nationwide .... Nationwide is on your side. (MUSIC OUT)

Nationwide TV Commercial (one minute)

1. (MUSIC UNDER) MOTHER: (VO) I love this house.

2. It was like an orphan when we adopted it...now it's adopted us.

3. I can't imagine living anywhere else.

4. And we won't ever have to because our mortgage has been paid off.

5. It's not that we're rich;

6. it's just that we had Mortgage Life Insurance from Nationwide when we needed it.

7. Eleven months ago, my husband died suddenly. It was an awful shock.

8. But it would have been so much worse if we'd had to move.

9. When our Nationwide Agent urged us to buy mortgage life insurance, I was against it.

10. It wasn't a big expense, but back then there were so many things I wanted more.

11. Things that seemed real to me.

12. But losing somebody is much more real.

13. Thank goodness my husband insisted on mortgage life when we bought our homeowners' insurance.

14. We'll always have our home.

15. ANNCR: (VO) Mortgage life insurance. It's part of Nationwide's blanket protection for your family.

16. SINGERS: Nationwide is on your side.... (MUSIC OUT)

Nationwide TV Commercial (one minute)

Irving Trust TV Commercial (30 seconds)

SFX: Cocktail Party Noises

MAN 1:   . . . and I need advice.

MAN 2:   You mean your accountant is talking about tax exempt bonds and you still don't have an Irving Trust Personal Banker?

WOMAN 1:   . . . money from an aunt, it came as quite a surprise.

WOMAN 2:   You mean you just inherited $250,000 and you still don't have a Personal Banker?

MAN 3:   . . . I cover the entire northeast.

MAN 4:   You mean your job is that important and you still don't have a Personal Banker?

Your own Personal Banker.

That's what makes
Irving Trust different

Irving Trust

ANNCR: If you're doing rather well, why settle for just a bank when you can have your own Personal Banker at Irving Trust?

A DARING USE OF HUMOR GAINS TOP RECOGNITION FOR A BANK'S PERSONAL SERVICE

Humor is a dangerous advertising tool. Nobody likes to be the butt of a joke, so when customers are made fun of, humorous ads can be counterproductive.

A successful approach is to humorously depict those who don't use the advertised service. That is what Irving Trust did in promoting its personal banking service. The danger of audience disenchantment was further shielded against and identification was increased by phrases in television commercials and headlines in print ads complimenting potential customers. Headlines in other ads included "You mean you're working out a financial plan, and you still don't have a Personal Banker?" and "You mean you need that much credit, and you still don't have a Personal Banker?"

TV commercials were placed on several New York stations adjacent to news or to selected sports, such as Wimbledon and U.S. Open tennis, to deliver the upscale and aspiring upscale audience, taking up about 75% of the budget.

Print was concentrated in *The New York Times* Sunday magazine.

Research, done by telephoning 6000 heads of households in nine New York State counties in and adjacent to New York City, showed that, despite being outspent by competitors by as much as 12 to 1, Irving Trust had the highest recall of "message slogan" and "personal service" among five major commercial banks in New York City:

	Bowery	Citibank	Irving Trust	Chase	Chemical	MHT
Message slogan	0.2%	8.3%	9.5%	4.9%	0.2%	0.8%
Personal service	0.6%	0.5%	4.5%	0.6%	0.6%	0.4%

The advertising agency was Brouillard Communications, a division of J. Walter Thompson Company.

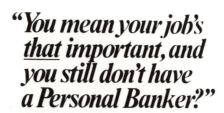

6

FINANCIAL DEALER-SUPPORT ADVERTISING

In a service industry, the quality and attitude of employees or dealers who talk directly to customers make a significant difference—can make or break a company. This may be even more critical in banking, investment, and insurance than in any other service industry. Discourtesy loses a customer, and customers often depend upon the officer, teller, account executive, agent, or other person for advice. Many of the transactions are not routine. All the transactions involve something about which customers have strong feelings—their money. A financial organization is not a dry-cleaning establishment.

For Chemical Bank many years ago, Doremus & Company developed a consumer advertising campaign based on the concept of "Gold Medal Service." Originally, the phrase had no validity. It was just words that might cause people to believe that they would get better service at Chemical than at other banks without making any statement that was untrue. A slide presentation informed employees about the campaign.

As the campaign continued, performance of employees improved, not only in the opinion of supervisors but also by the objective measure of written complaints, which dropped significantly. The employees had been motivated to live up to what was said about them in the advertising.

Account executives at brokerage firms and independent insurance agents and brokers can be affected even more by advertising aimed primarily at consumers.

Most account executives at brokerage firms, now sometimes called financial consultants or investment executives, and technically known as registered representatives, feel only a modest amount of loyalty to the firm for which they work. They are paid on commission—even those at Merrill Lynch nowadays— and most consider themselves independent businesspeople. A majority of those who have any amount of seniority have worked for more than one investment firm during their business lives, many for several. Often they leave because they don't like the manager of their office and/or because they are lured away by higher commissions, more services to offer, greater freedom, up-front payments, a more attractive location, or better clerical and secretarial support. Advertising ranks low among their consciously felt reasons for staying or leaving a firm, but it affects them more than they realize (see the E. F. Hutton case history in Chapter 7). Account executives who represent firms that prospects have never heard of labor under a big handicap. And when account executives become very successful, the psychic rewards of working for a well-known, highly regarded company can keep them content.

Those responsible for recruiting and managing account executives know this. More than one advertising campaign, carefully thought out by a highly competent agency and enthusiastically approved by the marketing people and other top management of the investment firm, has been dropped simply because the account executives didn't like it.

Advertising can also affect the specific investment that an account executive recommends when two or more investments meet a customer's requirements equally well. Consider John Nuveen & Company, for example, which markets tax-exempt unit trusts through account executives at brokerage firms. Nuveen, like many other independent sponsors of unit investment trusts, mutual funds, and other services sold through brokerage firms, does not deal directly with the investing public.

When an account executive decides that a tax-free unit investment trust suits the needs of a customer, or is asked to recommend one, the account executive usually has a choice of trusts to recommend. Often he or she can recommend a trust sponsored by his or her own firm. Merrill Lynch heads a group of investment firms that sponsors one, PaineWebber heads a group of investment firms that sponsors another, Advest and a third group sponsor a third.

As you can imagine, the managements of those firms would prefer that their account executives recommend the trusts they sponsor. Yet large numbers of account executives at Merrill Lynch, PaineWebber and other investment firms recommend a Nuveen trust instead, even though there is little difference between them. A big reason for this is the Nuveen advertising.

For many years Nuveen has been advertising directly to individual investors in *The Wall Street Journal, The New York Times* and other investor-read publications read by investors. Their newspaper ads usually dominate the pages on which they appear, and are often full pages. Each ad contains a coupon and a telephone number and meets all the principal requirements of direct response advertising but one: They are larger than would be most economical for producing leads at the lowest cost per lead, especially since the ads do not ask readers to send in money, but merely to send for more information. There's hardly anything more they need to know that is not in each ad.

The advertisements are larger because they are created as much to influence account executives at brokerage firms as to influence investors. Nuveen representatives pass along the leads from the advertising to account executives who want them. But many well-established account executives don't want them, even though the long copy pre-sells prospects so the leads are easier to convert into sales than leads from shorter ads would be.

To remind account executives of the advantages Nuveen trusts offer, the copy in the advertisements is longer than would be most efficient for direct response. Account executives today have so many services to sell that keeping the sales points of each in mind can't be easy. The Nuveen advertising periodically reminds them of the Nuveen benefits.

The advertisements must also be large in order to communicate the feeling that Nuveen is a big, solid firm—more or less equal in solidity to Merrill Lynch, PaineWebber, and other big investment firms. The account executives see the ads in *The Wall Street Journal* and other consumer publications and know that, because of the size and frequency of the ads, prospects will recognize and respect the Nuveen name when they mention it. The ads make account executives feel, correctly, that a Nuveen tax-free trust is an easy sale.

This policy, aided by direct mail, advertising directly to account executives in *Registered Representative* and *Financial Planner*, plus other measures conceived by Nuveen's marketing director, Donald R. Pitti, was responsible for a steady increase in Nuveen's sales and share of the market during the five years Benn & MacDonough was Nuveen's agency. At the end of the period, Nuveen's sales not only far exceeded those of all other independent sponsors of tax-free unit investment trusts combined, but were neck and neck with those of the leader—Merrill Lynch. Typical Nuveen advertisements are near the end of this chapter.

Many agents and brokers who sell fire and casualty insurance feel even more independent than account executives. Some insurance companies, such as Allstate, State Farm, and Nationwide, sell insurance only through agents who are full-time employees. But most fire and casualty insurance companies, such as CIGNA, sell insurance through independent insurance agents and brokers. These agents and brokers usually represent more than one company. They can recommend any policies they want to, depending on which they believe suit their client better, or for other reasons when there is little or no difference between the policies. Consequently, as was seen in the CIGNA case history, independent insurance agents and brokers constitute an important audience—maybe the most important audience—of what is ostensibly consumer insurance advertising.

Companies that don't sell insurance through independent agents and brokers, but only through their employee-salespeople, must advertise regularly in order to attract customers to their offices and to make their names recognized and welcomed when prospective customers are solicited in person or by direct mail. But insurance companies that sell through independent agents have a choice.

They can rely on communicating directly to agents and brokers by advertising in trade journals, direct mail, and personal calls, or they can supplement these efforts with consumer advertising.

In many respects, insurance companies that distribute through independent agents, and investment firms that distribute through account executives of other firms, can be likened to companies that sell drugs like aspirin through retailers. One approach, which keeps advertising costs down, is to concentrate on the retailer, providing counter displays and other aids and leaving a big margin between the suggested sales price and what must be paid the wholesaler.

The other approach is to force distribution through advertising. So much advertising is placed for the drug that customers come in and ask for the particular brand, Bayer Aspirin, for example. Because of this forced demand, the manufacturer does not need to offer the retailer the same big margin required of a supplier that does not advertise in consumer publications.

The choice, however, is not between no consumer advertising and a big consumer advertising budget like that for Bayer Aspirin or Nuveen. A little consumer advertising can go a long way. Dealer-support advertising does not need to be as frequent as advertising for an image campaign aimed primarily at consumers. Salespeople pay much more attention to the advertising of the products and services they sell than consumers do. It's their livelihood. So when they see an ad in a consumer magazine for what they sell, they give the ad much more weight than may be warranted. If Brand A runs, say, four ads a year in consumer publications, and Brand B runs none, which is the retailer most likely to sell, other factors being equal?

Many insurance companies follow this practice, putting most of their effort into influencing agents and brokers directly by placing an occasional ad in consumer publications. Competitors of Nuveen, and some mutual funds that are sold through brokerage firms, such as Chemical Fund, also follow this practice.

Which policy an independent provider of a financial service should follow depends upon a host of marketing factors. How big is the potential audience for the service? How much money can the provider of the financial service afford to risk on gaining sufficient additional sales to justify the sizable increase in the advertising budget? What is competition? No policy is universally better than another. The determination must be based on individual circumstances.

In any case, a firm that distributes its services through a sales force needs to consider the effect the advertising will have upon that sales force, whether the members of the sales force are entirely independent, full-time employees or in between. The more independent the sales force the more urgent the need to advertise and the more obvious the effect of the advertising.

Dealer-support advertising needs to be admired by the sales force. And since salespeople are not advertising experts (although nearly everybody considers himself or herself one), the efficiency of the advertising in appealing to consumers may need to be sacrificed to some degree. Small type crowded into a small space may pull the most returns per advertising dollars but may be counterproductive when the effect on the sales force is considered. Advertisements that appear "creative" to those who don't know advertising principles may affect the sales force more favorably than more subtly creative ads that have a greater effect upon consumers. Whatever the relative pulling power of the Nuveen ads that follow, the one with the illustration of the two people in bed was bound to be the more widely admired (which does not necessarily mean it pulled the most responses).

The principles of dealer-support advertising therefore affect the consumer advertising of all banks and most investment firms and insurance companies. These principles differ from what makes other consumer advertising most effective and efficient in the following ways:

1. Larger is better.
2. Frequency can be less.
3. Obvious creativity can be helpful.
4. Tasteful, admirable appearance is usually mandatory (larger type, white space, illustration, style).

WHICH UNIT INVESTMENT TRUST AD PULLED BETTER?

The two advertisements on the following pages appeared as an A–B split in a Sunday edition of The New York Times. Both were quarter-page ads. The principal differences are that one includes the return in the headline (which was relatively high at the time), while the other does not, but features a negative benefit. The copy in each is virtually identical. Which pulled the greater number of coupons and telephone calls?

The tax free income trust for New Yorkers who want to sleep nights

Interest income free of federal income tax, free of New York State tax, and free of New York City tax—that's what Nuveen's New York trust pays residents of New York State. This triple tax exemption can be of exceptional benefit. The current series of Nuveen's New York Trust pays 7.07%* tax free. To net this much after taxes, a New York State resident with taxable income of $24,600, filing a joint return, would need to find a taxable investment yielding 12.19%. A New York City resident would need to find an even higher taxable return.

Even more important, however, is the quality of the bonds in the Nuveen trust. Nuveen's New York Trust includes no bonds from Puerto Rico. And, of course, no New York City bonds. Every issue in the New York Trust meets Nuveen's stringent quality standards, besides being "A" rated by one of the established rating services. Nuveen has been specializing in municipal bonds since 1898, and is the largest sole sponsor of tax-exempt bond trusts with over $3 billion outstanding.

Interest income is payable monthly, quarterly, or semi-annually, as the investor chooses. Or it can be automatically reinvested in another Nuveen tax free fund, gaining the benefits of tax free compounding.

Units of the New York Trust can be redeemed at any time at no charge, and you receive full net asset value, which may be more or less than your purchase price.

For more complete information on the New York Trust, including charges and expenses, send for a prospectus on the Nuveen Tax-Exempt Bond Fund, Multi-State Series 4, by telephoning or mailing the coupon. Read it carefully before you invest or send money.

*This represents the net annual interest income, after annual expenses, divided by the public offering price as of 9/17/79. On 7/20/79 when Series 4 was first offered, the figure was 6.99%. It varies with changes in either amount and with the particular payment options. This figure is based on semi-annual payments.

Nobody knows municipal bonds like Nuveen

THE RESULTS

The ad with the return in the headline pulled well. It is a safe ad. The ad featuring the couple in bed was risky. It would have been foolhardy to place it extensively without testing. In the test it pulled spectacularly well. As a consequence, the "sleep nights" ad was placed extensively and continued to pull extraordinary responses wherever it was placed.

However, experience with other Nuveen ads showed that both ads would have pulled responses at a lower cost per response if they had been smaller. But then account executives at brokerage firms would not have been so impressed or so well informed about the Nuveen trusts.

7

HOW TO CHOOSE MEDIA FOR FINANCIAL ADVERTISING

In considering which media to use to influence individuals, the media person experienced in financial advertising considers the purpose of the advertising along with the demographics of the audience. Many even think about the purpose first.

If getting immediate action is the purpose, print—that is, newspapers and magazines—will usually be the most effective medium. But if the purpose is to increase awareness and/or to improve consumers' attitude toward the advertiser, television may be the most desirable.

Newspapers and magazines have proven their ability to gain suitable responses at a low cost per response for bank advertisers, for investment advertisers, and to a lesser extent for insurance advertisers. Because of finance's abstract nature, print can be more convincing than television. The numbers supporting the benefits can easily be shown, and readers can take all the time they need to ponder them and other supporting evidence. More information can be included, such as additional benefits and counters to objections, as well as the several addresses of the advertiser. A coupon can be used to stimulate replies. Print advertisements can be as short or as long as is most efficient. Even a single small-size ad can be effective. A budget of any size can be accommodated.

Even more important, people read financial sections of newspapers and financial magazines when they are concerned about their money. As they read the accompanying articles, they are thinking about where they can get the highest return or, if they need money, where they get money at the lowest rate. Depositors, borrowers, and investors are ready to respond.

Newspapers and magazines are the media to beat for financial direct response because the advertising can be more *convincing*, a ready-to-buy audience is *selected*, and the size of the ad is *adaptable* to any size budget.

Television, on the other hand, is the medium to beat for image advertising.

Television commercials can arouse more intense emotion and thus create greater favorable memorability—the qualities that are most desirable in an image campaign. Because of the combination of sight, sound, and movement, no other medium comes close to television, when its capabilities are fully exploited, in the power it can exercise over attitudes.

Especially important for image advertising, television forces itself on the viewer. Readers can easily skip newspaper and magazine advertisements, but viewers must exert themselves to avoid seeing and hearing a TV commercial. If the beginning of the commercial is well-conceived, they will stay to watch and listen.

These qualities make television ideal for image building because image advertising must reach people not only when they are ready to buy but also when they are not—which is most of the time. A favorable attitude needs to be built up so that when people do deposit or borrow money, or invest, or buy insurance or some other financial service, they will choose the advertiser, be amenable to a call or visit from the advertiser's representative, or welcome a recommendation that they buy a service provided by the advertiser.

A television commercial, because of its intrusiveness, will also reach another audience that is desirable for image purposes: those who can influence a prospect's choice of bank, brokerage firm, insurance company, or financial service— that is, friends, authorities, and other opinion-makers.

Television reaches a broad audience of prospects, eventual prospects, and influentials, and at its best makes them listen whether they have any current interest or not—and so influences their attitudes.

But the choice of which media to use is by no means clear-cut.

Several financial advertisers have successfully used newspapers and magazines to increase awareness and improve image. These media are usually chosen when the audience to be influenced is too narrow to make television economical.

And television—with the advent of cable—is increasingly being used for direct response. For example, Merrill Lynch turned to television when other measures failed to produce sufficient sales of a $1 billion mutual fund. The fund sold out in a few days. Manufacturers Hanover successfully sold certificates of deposit using television primarily. In both instances, the benefits were simple and strong: a much higher return on the mutual fund, and increased liquidity for the certificate of deposit.

Other media—radio, direct mail, and perhaps billboards—can be used effectively in financial advertising, but usually only as supplements to newspaper, television, and magazine advertising. Of the approximately $1 billion spent on commissionable financial advertising in 1983, newspapers took about 60%, television took 27%, and magazines took 11%. Network radio and outdoor advertising took only about 1% each. These figures do not include local radio or direct mail because expenditures for these categories are too difficult to collect.

In searching for case histories to include in this book, only one was found where success was attained by making radio the principal medium. That was the case history of National Enterprise Bank—more about that later in this chapter. Radio can't be as convincing or as selective as print, nor can it arouse emotion the way television can.

Few organizations can flourish with direct mail as their principal advertising medium. The only ones I know of are a few small discount brokerage firms. Direct mail costs too much when sent to a broad audience.

Direct mail pulls responses most efficiently when either or both of two conditions exist: (1) The audience is small. (2) A considerable amount of information will cause a profitable percentage of the audience to act as the advertiser wishes. See the Citibank case history at the end of this chapter and the AmeriTrust case history at the end of Chapter 2.

Billboards suffer from brevity—what can be said about a financial organization in six or seven words?—and from lack of selectivity.

However, experience indicates that placing advertising in more than one medium achieves results superior to that of overloading a single medium. Most of the successful case histories in this book involve two, three, four, or more kinds of media. One reason is the size of the budgets. After so much money is placed in one medium, a point of diminishing return is reached.

Another phenomenon is even more important. Advertising in more than one medium seems to affect those who are exposed to the same message even more strongly. Magazine publishers, for example, have found that direct mail pulls better when television commercials appear at the same time.

If experience did not indicate otherwise, one might think that a direct mail campaign and a TV direct response commercial with the same offer from the same advertiser would compete with each other, and that each would pull less well. But one actually helps the other. The net cost per response is lower.

Nobody knows for sure why this is so, but it may have to do with the natural instincts of humans and other animals. We check the stimulus we receive from one of our senses with another sense. A dog checks what he smells with his hearing and his sight. What humans hear (or smell) we also want to see.

The financial sections of local newspapers yield the best results for most bank and investment firms, partly because the prospects are local. In looking at the results of the case histories, however, people guiding the advertising of a bank or a regional investment firm need to consider the following fact: The effectiveness of the financial pages drops off fairly fast as the size and nature of the newspaper's circulation declines.

As measured by responses to investment advertisements, the cost-per-inquiry is lower in *The New York Times*, especially on Sundays, than any other non-national newspaper. Advertisements placed in the *Los Angeles Times*, the *San Francisco Chronicle*, the *Miami Herald*, and the *Chicago Tribune* are next best.

If the audience is national or is spread over a large region, national and regional newspapers, particularly the four editions of *The Wall Street Journal*, and magazines may be more efficient than local newspapers. Advertisements in *The Christian Science Monitor* often don't pull badly, perhaps because the audience is upscale and has confidence in the newspaper's advertisers. *USA Today* is too new to be evaluated at this writing.

Among national magazines, *Barron's* usually pulls responses for *investment* ads at a lower cost per response than any other—even at a lower cost than *The Wall Street Journal*. Three characteristics of *Barron's* may account for this. First, it is strictly about investing, not about business as well, as *The Wall Street Journal*, *The New York Times*, and most other leading magazines are. Second, many readers of *Barron's* are not subscribers, who receive it automatically, but buy it at newsstands. In other words, many buy it when they need to make an investment decision. Third, the cost of advertising space in *Barron's* is relatively low.

Investment advertisements pull well in *Forbes* and *Fortune*, and to a lesser extent in *BusinessWeek* and in some airline publications. The cost per response is usually significantly higher than in *Barron's*, because the circulations are greater and the audiences include many who read the publications for *business* or other reasons, not to help them make *investment* decisions. Among the newsweeklies, investment ads pull at a lower cost per response in *U.S. News & World Report*, again because the advertiser is not paying to reach so many people not able to invest or interested in investing.

Note that the above discussion is based on direct response advertising aimed at individual investors. If the advertising aims to improve image or is for bank or insurance services, or is aimed at businesses or other organizations, the relative efficiencies may be different.

For image advertising, publications with stable readerships—that is, from subscriptions—are to be preferred. Image advertising needs to be seen again and again by the same readers.

For bank and insurance services, strictly investor-oriented publications become less efficient, and newsweeklies and general publications become relatively more efficient. Note the use of *The New York Times* magazine in the Irving Trust case history at the end of Chapter 5. Income, rather than ownership of investments, becomes the criterion.

If prospects are businesses rather than individuals, then business readership becomes the criterion. Note the use of *The Wall Street Journal, Forbes, Fortune,* and *BusinessWeek* in the CIGNA case history in Chapter 1.

As a rule, trying to make financial advertising more effective by placing it in unusual media or in unusual ways wastes much or all of the advertiser's money. Direct response advertisements pull best in the media where the competition places advertising. Most media directors rightly leave beating the competition up to the creative people—most of the time.

The exceptions occur under special conditions, such as in the case history that follows.

RADIO ADVERTISING HELPS ESTABLISH A NEW BANK

National Enterprise Bank opened for business in downtown Washington, D.C., in September 1983. The bank was organized to provide specialized banking services to people in professional practices and in small-to-medium-sized businesses. The organizers themselves came almost entirely from this group.

The basic plan of the new bank was to operate from a single office in downtown Washington and provide deposit, investment, lending, and other services tailored specifically for the professional and business market to customers throughout the greater D.C. area. Telephone, messenger service, and personal visits were used to service customers so that busy professionals and businesspeople would not need to leave their offices to do their banking.

To help National Enterprise put its plan into action, the agency developed an advertising strategy that targeted this middle-market audience both demographically and psychographically. Radio was selected because of its ability to reach an upscale target with an action message at an efficient cost per impression. (The budget was modest.)

The stations and dayparts were carefully chosen after considerable research and investigation. They were WMAL-AM, owned and operated by ABC, which broadcasts news, talk, and middle-of-the-road music, and WTOP-AM, a CBS affiliate, which is all news. All commercials were scheduled during morning drive time.

The radio commercials were made from taped interviews with members of the bank's board of directors, who explained in their own words why Washington needed a new bank of this kind. The professions of each of the bank's spokespersons were identified, and they talked about how the bank could help people in that profession. Dentists talked about the help dentists could get, lawyers about the help lawyers could get, physicians talked to physicians, etc. This not only made the commercials convincing but also made the bank sound like one that professional and small-business people could identify with.

Radio was supplemented with full-page black and white ads in the regional edition of *BusinessWeek* plus ads in the professional and trade publications reaching physicians, dentists, lawyers, and accountants. In the print ads, tongue-in-cheek humor and slightly brash headlines and copy were used to appeal to the more sophisticated target audience and to establish a point of difference between this bank and its more established (and for the most part, stodgy) competitors.

The overall response to the campaign was tremendous. By the end of the

National Enterprise Bank Radio Commercial (one minute)

BILL: Dr. Jerome Sandler is a general surgeon in Landover Park and a director of National Enterprise Bank.

JERRY: . . . I spend a great deal of time in a teaching hospital educating residents, and it's very difficult for young people starting out in practice today to have any backing. They suddenly go out into the world and find that they have no credit anywhere. National Enterprise Bank understands this problem, and we want to encourage young physicians to come to our bank . . .

BILL: National Enterprise Bank. Member FDIC. Member Federal Reserve System.

JERRY: . . . Most of my friends who are in the medical profession are very interested in National Enterprise Bank, because we want to consider every doctor, every account, as a VIP. That's the whole concept. To give VIP service to the people that bank . . .

BILL: National Enterprise . . . the bank for professional and business people. 1722 Eye Street Northwest in downtown Washington. Phone 429–9888.

National Enterprise Bank Radio Commercial (one minute)

BILL: Hal Mesirow is managing partner of the Washington law offices of Lillick, McHose & Charles and a director of National Enterprise Bank.

HAL: In our work, we've got situations where we're going to be tied up for long periods of time in litigation and you need a bank that's going to follow through with you and take care of your problems and your needs. And you need a banking relationship that's a continuing one, that's ongoing. We are trying to approach the operation of National Enterprise Bank from the standpoint of a bank customer.

BILL: National Enterprise . . . the bank for professional and business people.

HAL: . . . My feeling is that we've got an ideal marriage shaping up here between an awful lot of professionals in this city and National Enterprise Bank, because we can do what these people want a bank to do.

BILL: National Enterprise Bank. Member FDIC. Member Federal Reserve System. 1722 Eye Street Northwest in downtown Washington. Phone 429–9888.

INTRODUCING COLLATERAL THAT'S RIGHT UNDER YOUR NOSE.

There's a new bank in town that knows how to make a dentist's life easier. With a full range of services. Including loans based on your income stream, not your balance sheet.

Since we look at what you earn, not at what you own, a healthy practice is all you need to qualify. Even if your practice is new.

We know how valuable your time is. So you can do your banking without ever leaving your office. Do it by telephone. By our prepaid mail plan. Or even by bonded messenger service.

Call Harry Felix, President, or Lee Donovan, Senior Vice President at National Enterprise. We make banking painless.

 **National Enterprise**

The bank for professional and business people.

1722 Eye Street/Washington, D.C. 20006 202/429-9888 Member FDIC/Member Federal Reserve System

91

tenth month in business, National Enterprise had taken in over $17 million in deposits and was projecting $20 million by the end of the first year of operations. Many new banks go for two and even three years before breaking into the black. But at National Enterprise, the volume of loans was such that the bank was operating at a profit by the end of the tenth month.

The agency was Gumpertz/Bentley/Fried.

In the National Enterprise case the budget was small and the creative solution depended upon the use of radio. While this exceptional media choice succeeded, similar choices involve considerable risk. One seldom hears about advertising placed in unconventional media or in unconventional ways that fail. Nobody publicizes it.

One common mistake made by inexperienced or ill-advised investment firms is to try to build an image or try to get responses by placing ads in sports or cultural magazines with high-income audiences. Because their readers are not thinking about investing at the time—because many people with high incomes spend all they make and have none left over for investing—this advertising consistently fails.

A similar common mistake is to place bank and investment advertising on newspaper sports pages. The logic is that men control most money decisions. But the advertising fails for the same reason that investment advertising fails in sports and cultural magazines—the audience doesn't want to think about money, and many readers don't have any money to deposit or invest.

Financial advertising has also failed several times when placed on the woman's page of newspapers, because: (1) Even now, men control much more money than women. (2) The news columns alongside the advertising are about fashion, children, health, and similar subjects, so readers are not thinking about money at that time.

Placing financial TV commercials on sports shows does not seem to suffer to the same degree, perhaps because (1) the principal purpose of the advertising is usually to increase awareness and (2) television advertising intrudes itself upon the viewer.

Or perhaps placing financial advertising on television sports shows does not seem relatively inefficient because nobody has rigorously tested news and news-type shows versus sports shows for financial advertising—or if they have, they have kept the results to themselves. Usually financial advertisers mix the two on TV, so the results cannot be determined.

Clearly, the closer any financial advertising is to similar editorial material, the better. And there are plenty of opportunities.

If the budget is small, small-space ads placed in the financial section of the local newspaper can be effective and efficient, as in the MBIA case history in Chapter 2. Direct mail can also be tailored to fit a small budget or used when the audience is specialized, as in one of the Citibank case histories at the end of this chapter.

Bigger budgets open up a host of possibilities: larger space on the financial pages of the local newspaper; regional and national editions of *The Wall Street Journal*; magazines to suit specialized audiences, as in the CIGNA case history in Chapter 1; or obtaining concentrated audiences, as in the Standard & Poor's investment advisory case history in Chapter 2.

Television becomes efficient if the budget is big enough for causing prospects to visit the office (as in the Connecticut Bank and Trust case history in Chapter 3 and other case histories that appear later in this book) or for increasing awareness and improving image, as in the case history that follows immediately.

TV PIONEERING REWARDS BROKERAGE FIRM HANDSOMELY[*]

In the 1950s and 1960s, E. F. Hutton was one of the steadiest and most successful direct response advertisers in the investment industry. Small-space coupon advertisements appeared weekly in newspapers across the nation. But a survey made in 1969 revealed that the firm's name was little known, even though E. F. Hutton ranked eighth in size among brokerage firms and had been in continuous existence under the same name since 1904. Even those who did recognize the Hutton name usually had no clear impression of the size and activities of the firm, some confusing it with another long-established investment firm with a similar name, W. E. Hutton.

Even before the survey was made, Hutton executives had sensed this and had taken their problem to Benton & Bowles, Inc. Executives of that agency were inclined to think that television would solve the problem of E. F. Hutton's near anonymity, based on their considerable experience with TV.

However, no investment firm used television at that time because the costs seemed high in relation to the then current advertising budgets of investment firms. TV's costs also seemed high in relation to the revenues of investment firms. In 1969, the number of shares traded on the New York Stock Exchange was about one-tenth the number of shares traded in the early 1980s.

Very prudently, therefore, Benton & Bowles recommended testing television against print in matched markets, a procedure common in package goods advertising but untried in investment marketing up until that time. Three pairs of markets with similar demographics were chosen, and the awareness ranking of E. F. Hutton was established in each. In one pair of cities, only television spots were used. In a second pair of cities, half-page coupon ads were placed in newspapers (the ads were five times larger than Hutton had been using). In the third pair of markets, as a control, the small coupon ads which Hutton traditionally used were placed in newspapers.

In six months, the results were clear. There was no change in the control markets, but in the markets where large newspaper ads appeared, awareness increased and attitude improved significantly. In the TV markets, however, awareness increased and attitude improved even faster and reached an even higher level.

But the high costs of placing enough television commercials to make a worthwhile difference remained. The budget had to be significantly less than a million dollars. The solution was limited placement in a limited number of markets. A flight of commercials was first placed in the markets where E. F. Hutton had the most account executives and where there was the greatest potential for growth: New York City, Los Angeles, and Chicago. Later the commercials were placed adjacent to news and sports shows in the firm's top 10 markets.

The commercials were constructed so as to affect the audiences that E. F. Hutton most wished to influence:

- *Individual investors*, with emphasis on those in higher-income brackets, who were in a position to invest at least $15,000

- *The financial community*, with focus on those who influenced institutional business

- *The business community*, especially the managerial levels (the influencers)

- *Account executives* and other employees of both E. F. Hutton and its competitors, as well as college seniors seeking a career in finance

Account executives were hardly the least important audience. Even a campaign which had as its only objective favorably influencing this audience would be highly effective, as revenues could be significantly increased through the improvement in morale, the gaining of additional customers brought to E. F. Hutton from other firms by account executives who shifted, and the upgrading in quality of E. F. Hutton account executives.

A slogan was created which, it was felt, would favorably influence all these audiences: "When E. F. Hutton talks, people listen." This line is a simple exposition of authority. It implies leadership and stature, reputation and reliability. It contains the company's name. It cuts across every line of finance. It is not restricted by daily variations in the stock market. It implies much about the company's employees. It made E. F. Hutton sound like the kind of firm most members of the target audience would want to identify with.

Note that the stress is more on identification than on benefits. If benefits were to be stressed, the slogan would have been something like "Hutton has ideas worth listening to."

The treatment of the basic theme derived in part from some early research conducted by the agency. Benton & Bowles had held focus group sessions with a diverse cross-section of active and potentially active investors. The principal purpose was to learn their subjective reactions to the advertising stances then taken by competing investment firms.

"One very useful thing we learned in these sessions," a B&B executive said, "was the use of humor in brokerage advertising. People didn't find anything funny about the investment of their hard-won dollars, but the reaction to just a touch of humor was favorable."

The commercials as created half-kidded the basic theme making the self-laudatory nature of the statement more acceptable. Further, the customer or potential customer was not laughed at. In fact, the E. F. Hutton customer was made to seem important and exclusive.

When E.F. Hutton talks, people listen.

A typical commercial opened with a long shot of a scene in a restaurant or back stage at a ballet or on a golf course or at some other upscale location where a number of people would naturally gather. One distinguished-looking man is talking to another, and nobody is paying any attention to them until one of the conversationalists says, "Well, my broker is E. F. Hutton. And E. F. Hutton says..." At the start of this line, every member of the cast stands stock-still and cocks an ear to hear what E. F. Hutton says. After a moment of silence, the announcer says, "When E. F. Hutton talks, people listen." The commercial ends with the E. F. Hutton logo and silence.

The television campaign, supported by large-space newspaper ads, continued for several years, with the budget increasing steadily. What were the results?

1. Five years after the campaign's initiation, awareness of the company among college-educated men with annual incomes of over $25,000 had gone from nearly zero to 97%. By 1980 it had gone to 99%.

2. At that same time, awareness of Hutton's advertising equaled Merrill Lynch's, and Merrill Lynch had been outspending E. F. Hutton by 4 to 1 for several years.

3. Correct identification of the Hutton slogan stood at 81%, almost twice that of the nearest competitor.

4. By virtually every criterion—"well-known," "able to fulfill investment needs," "experienced"—E. F. Hutton ranked in first or second position. And those characteristics had never been singled out for emphasis in the campaign. The slogan had endowed the firm with an entire range of positive attributes.

5. Quality account executives were attracted to the firm.

6. An internal survey showed that account executives appreciated being recognized and welcomed as representatives of E. F. Hutton when cold-calling.

7. Although other firms that merged (such as Shearson Lehman/American Express) later surpassed E. F. Hutton in size, by the late 1970s E. F. Hutton had climbed from eighth to second place in terms of revenues, without the benefit of a merger.

MULTIMILLIONAIRES SEND FOR A FREE BOOKLET ON GOLD BY CLIPPING A COUPON

Marketing people at the Bank of Boston (International) reasoned that if they could sell gold to wealthy people, the bank would profit not only from the sale and safekeeping fees but also from additional services to these new customers.

But how could leads be obtained? No list of multimillionaires all over the world exists. The bank brought its problem to Benn & MacDonough.

Market segmentation began on the largest possible scale. On what continent are there more prospects for a U.S. gold deposit service? The answer: South America.

The agency therefore advised placing an ad in magazines in South America and recommended appropriate publications based on analysis of the reading

Preocupados por la seguridad de su dinero, muchos inversionistas están dedicando parte del mismo a la compra de oro en los EE.UU. de A.

¿Por qué? Porque saben que los EE.UU. de A. es tanto el país políticamente más estable como el líder de las finanzas en el mundo entero. Así pues, nada tiene de coincidencial que en la ciudad de Nueva York se esté comprando ahora más oro que en cualquiera otra metrópolis del Globo.

Si Ud. se halla interesado en seguir tal ejemplo, nosotros podemos encargarnos de las respectivas transacciones en forma conveniente, eficaz, económica y, naturalmente, confidencial.

Sin embargo, las ventajas inherentes a su vinculación con nuestro Banco son mucho mayores que la representada por la simple diversificación geográfica de su capital. Creemos que no hay ningún Banco similar al nuestro en el mundo.

Una vez que Ud. acuda a nosotros, estará en comunicación directa con un Ejecutivo experimentado y diestro en materia de finanzas internacionales, obteniendo su asesoría confidencial ya sea mediante correspondencia, llamadas telefónicas o reuniones personales con él, tanto en su propio país como en la ciudad de Nueva York cuando Ud. viaje a ella. Tan experto banquero examinará con Ud. sus perspectivas financieras, aportando a su favor su vasto conocimiento acerca de las ventajas comparativas de mantener depósitos, solicitar préstamos o hacer inversiones prácticamente de cualquier modo posible en todo país donde ello sea viable.

El administrador de su cuenta personal no sólo aprovechará su pericia sino también la de sus competentes colegas bancarios en todo el mundo e inclusive la cooperación de nuestras facilidades especiales en Europa, el Caribe, Centroamérica y Asia.

Durante largo tiempo, nuestro Banco ha estado ayudando a la gente con el fin de que atienda de la mejor manera sus asuntos de dinero. En efecto, fue fundado en Boston (1784) cuando dicha ciudad era el centro financiero de los EE.UU. de A.

Tenemos la convicción de que ningún otro Banco estadounidense puede proporcionarle más servicios que el nuestro... pero, salvo que Ud. sepa de ellos y de todo cuanto nuestros expertos y especialistas conocen sobre finanzas internacionales, no podrá imaginarse lo que somos capaces de hacer por Ud.... Por otra parte, nos será imposible decirle cuáles de nuestros servicios lo beneficiarán, a menos que Ud. nos entere de lo que le interesa más. El Cupón adjunto le facilita esto. Basta que lo llene y nos lo envíe hoy mismo. Igualmente, si lo prefiere, puede escribirnos una carta explicándonos sus necesidades y circunstancias al respecto.

Lo anterior no implica costo u obligación para Ud. Nosotros podríamos indicarle medios de proteger su dinero que Ud. nunca pensó factibles.

Ogden White, Jr., President
Bank of Boston International (New York)
767 Fifth Avenue, New York, N.Y. 10022 — U.S.A.

Sírvase enviarme información sobre sus servicios bancarios internacionales para personas privadas, así como su folleto *"Purchasing Gold in the U.S.A."* ("Compra de oro en los EE.UU. de A."). Estoy particularmente interesado en:

☐ **Seguridad**

☐ **Seguridad más ganancia a largo plazo**

☐ **Seguridad más ganancia a corto plazo**

☐ **Préstamos en dólares u otras monedas**

☐ **Otro asunto:** _____

(Especificar)

NOMBRE: _____

DIRECCION: _____

Bank of Boston International (New York)
Subsidiaria de The First National Bank of Boston
767 Fifth Avenue, New York, N.Y. 10022 — U.S.A.
Teléfono: (212) 350-0300

Otras Oficinas — *EE.UU. de A.*: Boston, Los Angeles, Miami; *Suramérica y Centroamérica*: Avellaneda, Buenos Aires, Campiñas, Caracas, Ciudad de Guatemala, Ciudad de México, Ciudad de Panamá, La Paz, Montevideo, Nassau, Port-au-Prince, Porto Alegre, Río de Janeiro, Rosario, San José, Santa Cruz, Santiago, Santo Domingo, São Paulo; *Europa, Oriente Medio y Africa*: Beirut, Francfort, Ginebra, Guernsey, Londres, Luxemburgo, Madrid, París, Tehrán; *Asia y Oceanía*: Auckland, Bombay, Hong Kong, Manila, Melbourne, Singapur, Tokio.

Many investors concerned about the safety of their money are putting some into gold in the U.S.A.

They know that the United States of America is the most politically stable country in the world, as well as the world's financial leader. It is no coincidence that more gold is now bought in New York City than in any other city in the world.

If you're interested in following their example, we can handle your gold transactions conveniently, efficiently, economically and of course, confidentially.

But the benefits of your having a relationship with our bank go far beyond that of geographical diversification of your assets. There is, we believe, no other bank like us in the world.

You will have direct contact with a bank executive, experienced and skilled in international finance, once you establish a relationship with us. You get his confidential advice directly by letter, by telephone, and by personal meetings with him in your country and when you are in New York City. He will bring to bear on your financial situation a knowledge of the comparative advantages of maintaining deposits, borrowing, or investing in prac-

tically every possible form in every feasible country in the world.

Your personal account manager will draw not only upon his knowledge but also on that of fellow experts all over the world, including our special facilities in Europe, the Caribbean, Central America, and Asia.

We've been helping people with their money problems for a long time. We were founded in Boston in 1784 — when Boston was the financial center of the U.S.A.

No other bank in the U.S.A. can, we believe, provide you with more services than we can. Unless you know about these services and all that our experts and specialists know about international finance, you cannot imagine what we can do for you. And we can't tell you which of our services will benefit you unless you tell us what concerns you most. The coupon makes it easy. Mail it today.

If you prefer, write us a letter describing your needs and situation. There's no cost or obligation. We may tell you of ways to protect your money that you never thought possible.

audiences and the responsiveness of each. About half the small budget went into *Vision*, a Spanish and Portuguese language magazine similar to *BusinessWeek*. Ads were also placed in airline publications, mostly those of local airlines. The ads appeared in the language used in the publication, mostly Spanish, but also Portuguese and English.

As a consequence of a single insertion in each magazine, sufficient responses were pulled to justify sending an officer on a special trip to follow them up.

TARGETING ATM ADVERTISING AT SPECIFIC PROFESSIONALS GAINS MULTIPLE ACCOUNTS

Segmenting the audience for a service usually makes it possible to more effectively dramatize the benefits to each segment. The advertising can make the reader feel the benefit more strongly—as in the direct mailing which Citibank sent first to police officers and subsequently to other professionals such as doctors, nurses, and firefighters. All these professionals work odd hours, and consequently can benefit more than the average person from automated teller machines (ATMs).

Citibank sent 15,000 pieces to police officers in Long Island. The envelope had the teaser "Where can you bank at 4:30 in the morning?" Contents consisted of

- A folder
- Coupons that enabled recipients to get free checking, $25 off on a home appraisal fee, a $4 donation to a police charity, and $1 off on the first order of personalized checks
- Two signature cards for opening accounts
- A first-class business reply envelope

When the folder was opened, the reader saw a police shield and a Citicard in close juxtaposition, and the words "We're on the job—when *you* get off." The inside (shown on the next page) explained all the benefits police officers could get by opening a checking and savings account at Citibank. Included was a Customer Service Hot Line followed by the sentence "Someone will be there 24 hours a day."

The folder's back was headed, "Here's all you need to do to get started," followed by an explanation.

The return of 3% resulted in the opening of many multiple accounts relationships.

The agency was Mast Advertising Associates, Inc.

What makes Citicard Banking so perfect for Police Officers?

Well, 24-hour banking convenience combined with a Special FREE-CHECKING offer. Get instant cash, make deposits, make payments. Get greater control of your money than ever before.

Plus: Take advantage of the special offers enclosed with this brochure.

Thanks — I'll Do My Best To Help You. Just Follow With Me Step By Step

You can now get cash three ways . . . whenever you want it, day or night — 7 days a week

How Much Cash Would You Like?
$20
$30
$50
$75
More

- **From your Checking**
- **From your Citicard Savings**
- **From your Checking Plus line of credit**

Just press a few buttons. You can get your money in seconds at the Citicard Banking Center. You will like that extra convenience and it's all free!

You can now make sure that more of your money is earning interest — two ways!

The key here is Citicard Savings. When you have it, you can make sure you're always earning interest on all the money you can. Especially when Citicard Banking makes it so easy. Just push a few buttons at the Citicard Banking Center — you don't have to bother with any forms at all — and move money instantly from one part of your Citicard Account to another. For instance, instead of depositing your paycheck into your Checking, put it in your Day-to-Day Savings. Then . . .

Earn interest on your money right up until the time you want to pay your bills. Then shift only what you need to your Checking. The rest of your money will continue to earn interest from day of deposit to day of withdrawal.

Earn even more interest by keeping money you won't need for at least 90-Days in your 90-Day Savings.* Transferring money from Checking or Day-to-Day Savings to the higher interest 90-day Savings is a snap at the Citicard Banking Center. Or ask our Customer Service Assistants about our automatic way to earn more interest.

What else can you do at The Citicard Banking Centers?

Plenty!

Express Amount Of Deposit Or Payment

Deposits — Anytime! To your Checking or Citicard Savings.

Payments — Make payments on Checking Plus; Or on Ready Credit; Personal Loans, Mortgages or Master Charge and Visa, even on Christmas and Chanukah Clubs.

Receipts — Of course! Your Citicard Banking Center can give you a printed receipt for any transaction.

Information — On weekends, holidays, before, during and after regular banking hours, you can instantly check the balance in your Citicard Savings, Checking or Checking Plus Accounts.

Citicard Banking Center Phone

Use the Citicard Banking Centers with confidence. You'll soon find they're easy, exciting . . . and trouble-free. But should you ever have a problem, you can pick up the phone right next to the Citicard Banking Center and talk to someone who can assist you 24 hours a day.

As a Long Island Citibank customer you also get 24 hour "at home" assistance when you use our Customer Service Hot Line. Just call 516-752-5500 or 516-683-2100. Someone will be there 24 hours a day.

Citicard
h218 3040 532 00
RICHARD A HUNTER

8

HOW TO THINK CREATIVELY ABOUT FINANCIAL ADVERTISING

The process of creating original, constructive ideas is generally considered a mystery, but it's really quite easy to state. It consists of developing a set of parameters—that is, requirements or conditions—for a novel, a painting, a theory, an advertisement, or whatever, and then trying one idea after another, no matter how outrageous, until one fits.

That's what Albert Einstein did in creating the theory of relativity. He mentally persisted until he found a theory that fitted the parameters, that is, the observed facts and other proven theories.

George Bernard Shaw said about the principles governing the dramatist: "I do not select my methods; they are imposed upon me by a hundred considerations: by the physical considerations of theatrical representation, by the laws devised by the municipalities to guard against fires and other accidents to which theaters are liable, by the economics of theatrical commerce, by the nature and limits of the art of acting, by the capacity of the spectators for understanding what they see and hear, and by the accidental circumstances of the subject at hand." He goes on to list others, including "the rate of interest needed to tempt capitalists to face the risk of financing theaters."

The creative process is something like putting the first two pieces of a jigsaw puzzle together. One holds up the first piece, whose contours are the parameters, and then searches in one's mind for another piece whose contours fit the first. This is tiresome, at best, for many people, but it's exhilarating for some. It is impossible for anybody to use regularly in everyday life. Mostly we solve real-life problems by imitating what others do or by doing what has been done before. Reinventing the wheel wastes time and energy.

Most thinking is based on imitation. Creative thinking, therefore, is inherently unconventional—or turns out to be conventional, that is, similar to other solutions, only by a coincidence.

Judging and criticizing the creative work of others consists of knowing the parameters and seeing how well or how poorly the proposed solution fits—so not only copywriters and art directors, but also account people and advertising directors, need to know the parameters for financial advertising.

For creating or judging any advertisement, financial or not, the parameters can be classified as follows:

Purpose(s). What is the advertising expected to accomplish?

Audience(s). Who is to be affected by the advertising?

Subject. What is being advertised?

Competition. What similar services are being offered, and how?

Medium. How will the message be communicated?

Restrictions. What regulations, directives, and prejudices can result in proposed advertising being rejected even though it fits the other parameters?

We'll discuss the parameters one by one, even though a creative person's mind jumps from one to another and may take some for granted. And we'll discuss them first from the viewpoint of the copywriter, even though the creative process may involve interaction with the art director and other people. In subsequent chapters, we'll discuss the parameters from the viewpoint of the art director, account people, and the advertising director.

PURPOSE(S)

To develop an original, effective advertisement or commercial, the copywriter needs to think more precisely about what the advertising is supposed to accomplish than simply "direct response." If the purpose is to cause readers, viewers, or listeners to send in money, more convincing needs to be done than if they are just urged to get more information. People don't part with their money easily. If money is requested, objections usually need to be overcome, but if the purpose is to get sales leads, mentioning the objections may reduce the number of leads obtained. Some respondents won't have thought of objections until they hear them. When sales leads are the purpose, the writer can and should concentrate more on stimulating curiosity.

And even when obtaining sales leads is the purpose, the writer needs to know whether the marketing plan or method calls for obtaining the maximum number of leads possible or whether a smaller number of easier-to-convert or otherwise qualified leads is preferable. If qualified leads are desired, screens can be introduced into the copy. They may be overt, such as including a space in the coupon for the amount the respondent has available for investment, or the copy may be long so that prospects are pre-sold (both techniques were used in the Nuveen ads in Chapter 6).

If a free booklet is being offered, the maximum number of leads will be obtained by concentrating the copy on how helpful the booklet will be. But if qualified leads are the goal, emphasizing the service being offered, even including its price, will reduce the number of leads but increase the percentage that will be converted into sales.

Similarly, the more precisely the parameters are defined for image advertising, the more effective the advertising is likely to be. Is creating awareness more important than changing attitude? If awareness counts most, then a startling, memorable idea with little copy may be suitable. If changing attitude counts most, longer copy with a benefit headline may be preferable.

And while this book has emphasized that package goods techniques are usually wrong for financial advertising, sometimes, although rarely, accurate definition of the purpose makes package goods techniques suitable.

Consumers for one financial service, for example, made their choice of supplier in front of a computer screen. When they pressed a certain combination of keys, a number of suppliers appeared on the screen, many of them offering a service that was identical in every way at the same price. The consumers were like a housewife at a supermarket whose hand needed only to move a few feet in order to choose one brand over another, with little or no difference between the brands. In this instance, the prospect's fingers needed to move only inches. So the solution was advertising that emphasized the personal relationships the supplier had established with many prospects who were doing the choosing. Like package goods advertising, it concentrated on differentiating between brands in a memorable way.

Advertisements may have multiple purposes, like the early Merrill Lynch advertisements in Chapter 4 that needed to tell customers and potential customers regularly where the firm's offices were located, besides creating a distinctive image. Sometimes it is necessary to combine getting responses with creating image, as in the PaineWebber advertisements in Chapter 9. In fact, most financial ads even though primarily direct response or image, have a secondary aim that needs to be considered. A copywriter creating a consumer loan ad needs to keep the bank's overall image in mind, and few advertisers are adverse to having their image advertising result in some direct business.

AUDIENCE(S)

The more the copywriter knows about the nature of the audience or audiences the better. How much does the audience already know about the service being offered? And how homogeneous is that knowledge? Explaining the obvious will lose readers, as will neglecting to explain what is not known.

What is the attitude of the audience toward the service? If it is a fad, urging prospects to jump on the bandwagon may be the best advertising. If the audience has a negative attitude, their fears need to be quieted or overcome.

What is the financial status of prospects for the service? It's likely to be different for prospects for checking accounts than for prospects for municipal bonds or annuities.

Knowing the audience enables the skilled copywriter to make the reader, viewer or listener feel that advertising is addressed to him or her personally.

In direct mail, personally addressed letters pull best. Such precision is not possible in folders, booklets, and commissionable advertising, but the closer the message gets to the prospect's name the better. The direct mail folder at the end of Chapter 7 pulled so well because police officers were addressed by occupation. The National Enterprise Bank commercials, in the same chapter, succeeded in a similar way. One commercial named doctors, another dentists, another lawyers, another small-business people. So the truly creative copywriter considers such characteristics of the audience as occupation, interests, ages, sex, education, and family status. Remember the ''Give her the kitchen she deserves'' example in Chapter 3?

The copywriter also needs to consider the number of audiences that must be appealed to, plus any who will read the advertisement or see the commercial, especially those who meet customers, as discussed in Chapter 6.

When more than one customer audience needs to be influenced, and the benefits for each audience are different, creating separate advertisements for each will usually be most effective. But sometimes separate ads are not feasible. Each of the split audiences may be too small to justify an individual ad. Then the copywriter has a problem. A solution for advertising by a corporate income trust was to list and picture the various audiences who could benefit: a pension plan administrator, a self-employed person, a retired couple, an employee in a company without a pension plan, an employee who had just received a pension or profit-sharing check, and somebody who wanted a relatively high income. They were asked to send for a booklet that described the benefits to each in detail. The ad pulled extraordinarily well.

SUBJECT

Is the service new? That's usually the first question an experienced copywriter asks. If it's new, featuring its newness will usually increase the effectiveness of the advertisement or commercial. ''New,'' ''now,'' ''announcing,'' and ''introducing'' are all words that increase returns to direct response advertisements and the readership of image advertisements.

If the service is not new, reviewing previous advertising for the service—and the results of that advertising—can be helpful. If the previous advertising has not been successful, determining the reason demands first priority. This is usually easier than figuring out how to create advertising that will be more successful than already successful advertising.

Next, or concurrently, the experienced copywriter looks for material benefits. If the service requires a deposit, an investment, or a payment, the copywriter asks, What is the likely return? What tax savings are there, if any? How convenient is it? How liquid is it? How much risk is involved? Does it offer any other advantages?

For loans, What is the interest and other costs? is substituted for What is the likely return? If the bank, investment firm, insurance company, or other financial organization is the subject of the advertisement, the questions are simply generalized.

Next, or concurrently, the copywriter looks for psychological benefits—that is, what other desirable emotion can be elicited in prospects other than that which will result from their receiving one or more material benefits?

For example, many people want to identify with the biggest and the best. The emotional identification goes beyond their getting the logical benefits of safety and service that dealing with the biggest and best may provide. They want to deal with the biggest and the best because it suits their concept of themselves as superior people. They've arrived.

A minority of people feel the opposite, but even they are numerous enough for identification with the underdog to be a possible psychological benefit, as in the Avis "We try harder" campaign.

Mutual funds that tailor their investments to suit moral or political attitudes, such as not investing in companies that maintain plants in the Republic of South Africa, feature a psychological benefit.

Psychological benefits become especially important when the person who purchases the financial service does not receive the material benefits, as in life insurance and some loans. The Nationwide advertising in Chapter 5 gives fathers the psychological benefit of demonstrating their love by buying life insurance. The husbands who took out home improvement loans in order to "Give her the kitchen she deserves" gained a psychological benefit.

Despite these successes, psychological benefits as a rule pull fewer returns and are otherwise less effective in financial advertising than material benefits. Perhaps psychological benefits are harder to develop and riskier to use. Or perhaps people's desire to make or save money is so strong that other benefits pale beside them. Patriotism, for example, fails as an offered benefit for buying government bonds except in wartime.

Many advertisements and direct mail pieces on estate planning make the mistake of featuring how much fuss will occur after the prospect dies if he or she does not arrange the estate neatly. Accenting the material benefits the prospect will obtain while alive will usually do much better. One brokerage firm repeatedly ran an ad for its Florida office with the headline "More income for you now and more money for your heirs may be possible." The returns were so great that the manager said most of the revenues of his office resulted from the ad. Note that the material benefit to the purchaser came first in the headline.

In analyzing the subject, the copywriter needs to relate its characteristics to the audience. What counts most is finding or developing a benefit or benefits, material or psychological or both, that fulfill the emotional and logical needs of a sizable number of prospects.

COMPETITION

Who is the competition? The answer to this question can make a big difference in the effectiveness of the advertising—and it's not always obvious. The headline

"We believe we save investors more money than any other discount broker" presumed that the competition was other discount brokers—but it was not, so far as the advertising was concerned. Competitors are those the advertiser aims to take business away from—or who can take business away from the advertiser. The biggest source of business for discount brokers at that time was Merrill Lynch and other full-price brokers, not discount brokers. Other discount brokers were not likely to take business away from the advertisers, and the advertisers could take very little business away from them. That's another reason why the headline "You can save $1225.80 in brokerage commissions" pulled better— it competed with the full-price brokers.

The early Merrill Lynch and Paine, Webber, Jackson & Curtis advertisements recognized that their principal competitors were not other brokers—not even each other—but banks and insurance companies. Merrill Lynch and Paine, Webber needed to cause people to put some of their extra money into common stocks, not into savings accounts or insurance policies.

Consider the ATM advertising for Connecticut Bank and Trust Company (CBT), in Chapter 3, and the ATM advertising for Citizens & Southern National Bank, at the end of this chapter. Their advertising differs radically because the competitive situation was different.

CBT recognized that the competition was teller services, mostly at their own offices. Consequently, the benefit contrasted the two kinds of service to ATMs great advantage. Citizens and Southern (C&S) needed to compete with the ATMs of other banks, so a psychological benefit was used to enhance the superiority of C&S's ATMs.

Once the competition is established, the next question is "Are we David or Goliath?" If the advertiser is Goliath, the best kind of advertising may emphasize Goliath's leadership, like the advertising for Morgan Guaranty at the end of Chapter 4. But if we are David, we need to find a chink in Goliath's armor. Often in financial advertising the chink is "personal service," as in Irving Trust's advertising (Chapter 5) and National Enterprise's advertising (Chapter 7). But there are countless other possibilities. See the PaineWebber advertising near the end of Chapter 9, for example.

MEDIUM

Just as TV might be called the natural medium for package goods, so print is the natural medium for financial services. The benefits, concepts, and explanations of financial services can best be communicated in words—not pictures— because of the abstract nature of finance. Percentages and numbers can be used in print without confusing prospects. Prospects can read at their own pace. And they can re-read, which is a big advantage, because most financial services are not bought on impulse but after considerable thought.

In writing for TV, the copywriter needs to keep in mind television's limitations. Percentages and other numbers need to be kept to a minimum. And the entire commercial needs to be simple and strongly unified. Television is "natural" for package goods because package goods advertising requires communication of one big, simple, emotional idea. Note how the TV commercials in the case histories in this book follow this precept.

Radio is even more limiting, but both radio and TV have certain advantages that print does not have, which the creative copywriter can exploit. The National Enterprise commercials communicate an attitude of personal attention by using actual voices of the directors of the bank—making the message more convincing than would be possible in any print advertisement. The feeling of love between the father and son in the Nationwide commercials (Chapter 5) could not be approached in print.

The medium also affects the type of benefit and the outline of the message. A direct response print ad usually follows the Benefit-Conviction-Action-desired formula. A television commercial may follow this outline as well, but it more often follows a short-story outline and puts the benefit in a negative form initially. The reason is this: A print advertisement needs to *attract* the appropriate audience, while a television commercial needs to *hold* the audience that is already there. The short-story formula has proven over the centuries to be the best form for holding an audience's attention. It consists of establishing an empathetic hero, putting him in trouble, and then getting him out.

Consider the Connecticut Bank and Trust television commercial in Chapter 3. It opens with a person like the viewer (hence an empathetic hero) hammering on the doors of a bank. The voice emphasizes the trouble he is in: "Ever notice when you need cash the most . . . "

Early in a Merrill Lynch direct response commercial the hero's face drops when after he states that he got 12% on a recent investment he is told he could have gotten 15%. He's put further in the hole by being told, "Yours isn't backed by the government. Ah, too bad." But Merrill Lynch saves him in the end by telling him he can still call.

All in all, television is more flexible than print. Because of the holding power of a person in trouble, successful TV commercials may use this dramatic technique without following the short-story outline. TV commercials may also use poetic techniques, as in the Nationwide commercials.

Creative copywriters fully utilize the advantages of the medium in which they are asked to communicate.

RESTRICTIONS

Inexperienced copywriters rage against arbitrary restrictions on their creativity, but experienced copywriters take legal and other restraints as a matter of course and deal with them as part of the creative process. No method of communicating is without what seem to be arbitrary restraints of one kind or another. Remember the George Bernard Shaw quote at the beginning of this chapter?

Sometimes these restrictions can be turned into an advantage. For example, regulators of investment advertising often require that risk be discussed so that the ad will not be misleading. John Bodnar, at one time a copywriter at Benn

& MacDonough, knew that many people invest partly, and a few people primarily, for excitement, so he wrote the headline "Ten Risk Stocks" for a brokerage ad offering a booklet containing growth stocks the firm recommended. The ad pulled extremely well.

Similarly, mutual fund ads that tell how well the fund has performed should usually also state that past performance cannot be taken as an indication of future performance. I put words to this effect in the headline and added the subhead "It may be much better." The ad pulled very well.

The most confining restrictions in financial advertising apply to tombstones offering new issues of securities. The next most severe are those affecting investment companies (the legal term which includes mutual funds, unit investment trusts, and investment trust certificates). For other services, the regulations of the New York Stock Exchange, the National Association of Securities Dealers, and similar investment organizations are relatively easy to follow. As are the regulations applying to bank and insurance advertising.

A copywriter needs to become expert on the legal restraints that apply to the type of advertising he or she is creating. Time and time again, advertisers have hired an agency with no knowledge of the legalities and said, "Go ahead and just create. We'll modify your advertising to meet the requirements." It has never worked, as anyone who understands the creative process would know.

It's even good for a copywriter to know not only the regulations, but also the current attitude of the regulators toward the regulations. It's something like the Sunday blue laws in most communities: A retailer must know whether the police are enforcing the laws or not.

All the restraints on a copywriter are not legal, however. The copywriter may be faced with prejudices or directives from the account executive or the advertising manager which he or she believes hamper creativity without justification. The experienced copywriter does not necessarily take these as established parameters. He or she may create advertising that violates these restrictions and try to persuade those who must take the responsibility for them that the restrictions are wrong or unnecessary. Or he or she may take them as valid parameters. There is no easy answer.

Some agencies have the policy that what pleases the executives at the client company is good advertising. This works if the executives at the client company are advertising experts and know more than the agency people.

Some agencies have the policy of creating what they believe is best for the advertiser, and then persuading the advertiser that it is the best.

Both policies work at times and fail at times. The copywriter needs to adapt to the policy of his or her agency or find one that suits him or her better.

TO SUM UP

Once the facts about purpose, audience, subject, medium, competition, and restrictions have been established, the creative person hunts for the uniquely appropriate idea that fits the mold that has been established.

In the next chapter we'll see how a successful copywriter finds the appropriate idea, but first let's look at a case history that illustrates how a change in the parameters affects the creative solution.

HUNDREDS OF MILLIONS OF DOLLARS PULLED INTO A CMA COMPETITOR IN JUST THREE MONTHS

As the stock market began to rise in 1983, money began drifting out of Fidelity's long-established, large money market fund—Fidelity Daily Income Trust. To retain the money in one form or another, and to profit from its being invested in securities, Fidelity created Fidelity USA, a service similar to Merrill Lynch's Cash Management Account (CMA), but superior in several respects.

Once Fidelity USA was functioning properly, Fidelity Marketing Vice President Rob Legasey decided to go on the offensive. Since Merrill Lynch had acquired a sizable percentage of those who were possible prospects—perhaps 90%—comparative advertising made sense, and the ad on the following page was created by copywriter Paul Pedulla, art director Andy Simko, and creative director Bob Linderman, all of Cabot Direct Marketing.

What holder of a Merrill Lynch CMA account could avoid reading the copy once he or she opened the newspaper or magazine to this page? The illustration, supported by the headline, exploits two human tendencies. One is for people to pay more attention to the advertising for a service or product *after* they have bought it than before. This characteristic may spring from people's strong identification with anything they own, the fear of having made a mistake, or a desire to be reassured. In any case, it's a fact, so anybody holding a CMA account is likely to pay attention to any ad in which CMA is prominently displayed—particularly if the display is provocative, as in this ad.

The illustration and headline obtains the reader's attention, sparks his or her interest, and arouses his or her feelings of fear and/or hope. The copy convinces the reader of the superiority of Fidelity USA with factual, easy to comprehend comparisons.

The full-page ad, at a cost of $60,000 per insertion, was placed 15 times in *The Wall Street Journal*. It was also placed two additional times in just the Eastern edition, twice in *Barron's*, twice in *Money* magazine, and once in *The New York Times*.

The day the ad first appeared in the national edition of *The Wall Street Journal*, nearly 1000 telephone replies were received—before noon! Hundreds of coupons followed.

The inquiries still needed to be converted into sales. The first, essential step in marketing procedures of this kind is to send out information promptly, while prospects can still remember what they sent for and while they are

Fidelity USA is getting a herd of new customers.

Because Fidelity USA made a bullish idea better by offering up to 70% commission savings when you buy or sell stocks. And every day more CMA' customers are agreeing with us. They're comparing asset management accounts and finding a better value in Fidelity USA.

Here's what they discovered:

CMA	USA
Customer questions shunted to different departments	One salaried customer service rep stays with you, answers all questions via one toll-free phone call
Debit credit card without float	Gold MasterCard with very attractive float
All cash spendable via writing checks	Invested savings kept separate from checking balance
Daily sweep $1000 or more	Daily sweep $500 or more
Full commissions on stock purchases and sales	Up to 70% savings on your stock transactions
No cancelled checks returned unless individually requested	All cancelled checks returned to you
No pay-by-phone service No bill payment service	Recurring bills paid automatically; pay-by-phone for other bills

Here's how Fidelity USA works:
A minimum initial investment of only $10,000 (or $20,000 in securities) qualifies you for *all* of Fidelity USA's financial services and benefits.

You can write as many checks as you want for any amount in your account. Your available cash is invested in Fidelity Daily Income Trust (FDIT) and earns at money market yields.

And you can buy or sell stocks at commission savings of up to 70% through Fidelity Brokerage Services.

Your Fidelity gold MasterCard lets you get cash, goods and services worldwide. And you can pay bills by phone or arrange for Fidelity to pay them automatically on specified dates.

At tax time, your Fidelity USA statements give you a complete record of the year's financial transactions.

Fidelity USA: It puts it all together.

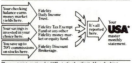

Plus you get international gold MasterCard, unlimited free checking, time-saving pay-bills-by-phone, coded cancelled checks for easy tax reporting, many other benefits all for a small monthly fee, tax-deductible!

You're also free to set apart money in your Fidelity USA and use it as savings in any Fidelity Money Market or Equity Fund. Or put it in TEMMT, our Tax Exempt Money Market Trust.

One customers-only toll-free number lets you do all your business and get straight answers to any questions, instantly.

Here's how easy Fidelity USA is to open:
It's easy and inexpensive (just $3 a month*) to have an asset management account that does more for your money. Call our toll-free number for more information on how the Fidelity USA can be your personal business manager.

*There is an added charge of $36 a year for gold MasterCard.

Call today!
Toll-free 1-800-225-6190
In Mass. call collect (617) 523-1919

YES, please send me information about the exciting new Fidelity USA account, including an FDIT prospectus, management fees and expenses. I will read it carefully before investing or sending money. I understand the minimum investment is $10,000.

Name _____
Address _____
City _____
State _____ Zip _____
Daytime Phone _____

Fidelity Group P.O. Box 832
82 Devonshire Street Boston, MA 02103

Fidelity Offices: Atlanta, GA; Austin, TX; Beaumont, TX; Boston, MA; Chicago, IL; Clearwater, FL; Cleveland, OH; Dallas, TX; Denver, CO; Garden City, NY; Houston, TX; Kansas City, MO; Los Angeles, CA; Miami, FL; Naples, FL; New York, NY; New Orleans, LA; Paramus, NJ; Phoenix, AZ; St. Louis, MO; San Francisco, CA; San Jose, CA; Sarasota, FL; Seattle, WA; Tulsa, OK.

Switch to Fidelity USA.

CMA is a registered trademark of Merrill Lynch.

still emotionally receptive. Fidelity sent out the direct mail conversion package, first class, within 48 hours of receipt of a telephone call or coupon.

The direct mail package differed from the advertisement in several respects because the parameters were different. Since the medium was direct mail, Jack Dickerson of Dickerson Inc. and his colleagues, copywriter Derald Brenneman and photographer John Van S., could say and show much more, and do so in color.

The restrictions were also different. The creators of the direct mail package could also discuss subjects and describe benefits that the ad could not because of regulations of the Securities and Exchange Commission and the National Association of Securities Dealers. The achievement in writing the ad can be appreciated only by those who know the severe regulatory restraints under which the creators of the ad were laboring—discussed in Part Two of this book. It is enough to say here that additional topics could be discussed in the direct mail package because a prospectus fully describing the mutual funds involved was included in a pocket in the back cover of the booklet.

Most important, the purpose of the direct mail package was no longer to create dissatisfaction among Merrill Lynch clients, but to overcome their inertia. They needed to be caused to want Fidelity USA so much that they would fill out the application and mail a check for at least $10,000.

Consequently, the comparisons so vital to the space advertisement were missing entirely from the direct mail package. Merrill Lynch and CMA were not even mentioned. Instead, the copy and art concentrated on material and psychological benefits. The entire mailing piece was handsome, so that Fidelity USA instantly became a service with which the necessarily upscale prospects would want to identify.

Only the cover of the 9″ × 12″ envelope had any relation to the advertisement. Along the bottom of the attractive gold and maroon envelope was the statement "This is the cash management account you've been waiting for. The account so many are switching to."

The cover of the 12-page booklet immediately appealed to the reader's pleasure at having his or her self-esteem increased. The reader first sees in large, graceful type, the words "Portrait of a Modern Success" followed by a big space and then "(You)." Then he or she sees at the top in smaller type "Fidelity USA presents. . . . "

The first paragraphs of the copy immediately put the reader in a hole by emphasizing his or her problems as an owner of several different securities issues and as an active investor:

"You expected to pay a price for success, but nobody told you about the avalanche of financial details."

"If you're like most successful people, trying to keep on top of things . . ." etc.

The next page is a full-page, full-color photograph of a man working at his desk on the details of managing his securities. The photograph is not exaggerated or funny, but direct and realistic. Copy is on the opposite page. The next page shows a full-page, full-color photograph of another man, relaxed and holding a Fidelity USA report. The rest of the booklet carefully and fully explains the many advantages offered by Fidelity USA, going into more detail and including an actual report with clear descriptions of each item.

In the pocket in the back is an easy-to-fill-out New Account Application. There are boxes to check next to several statements, including "Please send me a form to transfer my account from another broker."

The cost of each of the first 50,000 direct mail packages was $2.01; postage was $1.05 each.

Cash and securities worth more than $300 million were deposited in Fidelity USA in the first three months of the campaign. In its first year, the program attracted over $1 billion in assets.

9

HOW TO WRITE FINANCIAL ADVERTISING

Strange as it may sound, creativity in advertising is founded on what has worked before, but it is not imitative. The successful copywriter draws upon techniques that have been successful in the past and on his or her knowledge of human nature.

To be successful, the copywriter needs to know what arouses people's interest, what convinces them, what changes their attitudes, what causes them to act— knowledge the copywriter has gained through personal observance of people and their actions, through studying what experts have to say on the subject, and through drawing generalizations, establishing hypotheses, putting them into practice, and seeing what succeeds and what fails.

The successful copywriter draws upon everything he or she has discovered about influencing human beings. He or she knows how intensely people are interested in themselves, and that this interest is much stronger than is generally acknowledged. That's why it is virtually impossible to overdo the use of "you" in an advertisement or commercial. The successful copywriter knows that when the use of "you" is inappropriate every effort needs to be made to cause the reader, viewer, or listener to feel that his or her needs, wants, and desires are being discussed.

The experienced financial copywriter also knows that people are intensely concerned about money—about getting more and protecting what they have. Nobody is fooled by the cliché "Money can't buy happiness." Every sane person knows money provides people with opportunities not only for happiness but also for power and fulfillment. The more money a person has, the greater that person's freedom.

The third key fact about people that the successful financial copywriter knows is that people are motivated to act and to change their attitudes not by logic but by emotion. Most financial advertising succeeds by arousing either or both of two emotions: hope and fear. See the facing page for examples.

Occasionally other emotions are aroused by successful financial advertisers, such as anger, especially when money is not involved in the benefit. Examples include the CIGNA peanut ad (Chapter 1) and the Connecticut Bank and Trust ATM commercial (Chapter 3).

This is not to say that logic means nothing in financial advertising. On the contrary, the art of financial advertising often is to cause the reader, viewer or listener to believe he or she is being guided by logic, not by emotion. Put another way, financial advertisements must seem logical, because raw or obvious emotion-arousing techniques may cause prospects to feel they are being flim-flammed. Financial copywriting is an "art that conceals art."

If a copywriter discovers from analysis of the subject, the audience, and the competition that a strong, competitive benefit can be featured, little more thinking about the direction of the advertising need be done. Dramatizing that benefit—making the audience *feel* how good it would be to have it—becomes the copywriter's task. One example is "You can save $1,225.80 a year in brokerage commissions" (before Chapter 1). Another example is the advertising campaign for the Union Trust MasterCard, described next.

DRAMATIZING A STRONG, COMPETITIVE BENEFIT MORE THAN DOUBLES CREDIT CARD ACCOUNTS

Consumers think of credit cards as being pretty much the same, and most carry a card issued by the bank where they maintain a checking and/or savings account. Greediness of competitors, however, created a potentially strong, competitive difference for credit cards issued by Union Trust Bank of Maryland.

Maryland did not allow an annual fee on credit cards in 1982, so early in that year the four major competitors of Union Trust moved their credit card headquarters to Delaware to be able to enforce an annual fee.

Research showed that consumers resented both the fee and the loss of jobs in the state. Union Trust decided to keep its headquarters in Maryland and to continue a no-annual-fee policy.

To fully capitalize on the distinctive advantage of a no-fee MasterCard and to generate further awareness of Union Trust, the card was offered as part of a banking package. To receive the no-fee MasterCard, the consumer had to open a Union Trust checking account with a $300 minimum savings account. The checking account was then promoted as a no-charge checking account in coordination with the no-fee MasterCard.

**The Most Common Emotions Aroused or Quieted
by Successful Financial Advertising**

Hopes	Examples
Getting more money	"A checking account that pays like an investment." "When E. F. Hutton talks, people listen."
Saving money	"You can save $1225.80 a year in brokerage commissions." "This car cost $500 more at Security Pacific."
Improving self-regard	"You mean your job's that important and you still don't have a personal banker?" "You'd be amazed at how easy it is to be a Financial Wizard."
Gaining love	"Give her the kitchen she deserves."
Gaining immortality	"To help make sure he's taken care of until he can take care of himself."
Excitement	"Ten risk stocks."

Fears	
Losing money	"The tax-free investment for New Yorkers who want to sleep nights."
That money will lose its purchasing power	"Many investors concerned about the safety of their money are putting some into gold in the U.S.A."
Being ashamed	"How to feel comfortable during the uncomfortable process of getting a loan."
Envy (fear of not getting benefits other people are getting)	"Fidelity USA is getting a herd of new customers."

In the first year of the campaign, there was a 42% increase in the number of new consumer checking accounts and a 151% increase in new MasterCard accounts. Ketchum Advertising was the agency.

Union Trust TV Commercial (30 seconds)

Video	Audio
Open on MasterCards in a Line—Domino Effect. In Slow Motion Cards Fall.	SFX: Falling Cards (Amplified)
	ANNCR: (VO) First just a few banks in Maryland charged an annual fee on their MasterCard.
	Now it seems to be contagious.
	And you've got no guarantee your MasterCard won't be next.
Camera Cuts To Standing U.T. MasterCard	Unless it's this one.
	The Union Trust MasterCard.
Cut Back To Cards Falling	If you open a MasterCard account any-
Cut Back to Standing U.T. MasterCard	time between now and September 29,
Super: No-Charge Checking Account Needed	Union Trust will guarantee
Cut Back To Cards Falling	you'll pay no fee until at least 1987.
Super: 3 Years No Fee Guaranteed	For a MasterCard with no fee, guaranteed.
Union Trust Logo	Simply switch to Union Trust.
We Make Money Matters Simple	

Union Trust Radio Commercial (30 seconds)

ANNCR (VO):	First just a few banks in Maryland charged an annual fee on their MasterCard.
SFX:	Amplified sound of cards falling
ANNCR (VO):	Now it seems to be contagious
SFX:	Sound of cards falling in rapid succession
ANNCR (VO):	And you have no guarantee your MasterCard won't be next. Unless . . .
SFX:	Music Fanfare
ANNCR (VO):	It's the *Union Trust* MasterCard. All that's required is you open a no charge checking account with *your* MasterCard account anytime between now and September 29. Union Trust will guarantee you'll pay no fee until at least 1987. For a MasterCard with no fee, guaranteed for three years, simply switch to Union Trust Bank. Member FDIC.

But what if the distinctive benefit is not strong—or if there is no distinctive benefit at all? A slight benefit may be enhanced by adding a psychological benefit.

MAKING THE USER A HERO ENHANCES ATM PRODUCT SUPERIORITY

Sometimes not being first with a new product or service can be the best strategy for success—so long as there's total commitment to success.

In 1973, Citizens and Southern National Bank of South Carolina (C&S) began studying automated teller machine (ATM) programs and their impact on consumer banking. While other banks around the nation hurried to get machines out in the marketplace, C&S made a decision to thoroughly examine ATM hardware and software with the objective of installing a system that would have longevity and flexibility.

In late 1976, two of C&S's major (larger) competitors introduced off-line ATMs in South Carolina. Both competitors used heavy advertising to promote ATM awareness.

The reaction of C&S was to continue to work toward long-term success. A decision was made to bring up the C&S ATMs on-line, meaning the machines would have greater service capacity and more services for consumers. From the beginning sessions, the ATM planning committee was comprised of operations, data processing, branch administration, and marketing personnel. As a result, when C&S introduced ATMs in Columbia, South Carolina, in the fall of 1977, the program behind the introduction was a comprehensive one, totally involving all the various responsibility centers.

The on-line system for C&S ATMs sparked ideas for a unique approach to marketing them. The system would allow users to conduct a variety of banking transactions beyond the usual cash withdrawals. Transferring of funds between accounts, determining balances, and making loan and charge card payments could all be done at a C&S ATM. With this in mind, the bank's advertising agency, Bozell & Jacobs (B&J), proposed that the ATM itself should not be the hero, but rather that the customer, who by using it was doing incredible things with his money, should be the hero. Therefore, B&J recommended naming the *users* "Financial Wizards."

When the machines were installed, a mirror inscribed with the words "You're looking at a Financial Wizard" was affixed to the vandal shield. The bank staged energetic kickoff meetings and established an incentive program to encourage selling customers on the advantages of becoming a Financial Wizard.

You'd be amazed how easy it is to become a Financial Wizard.^{SM}

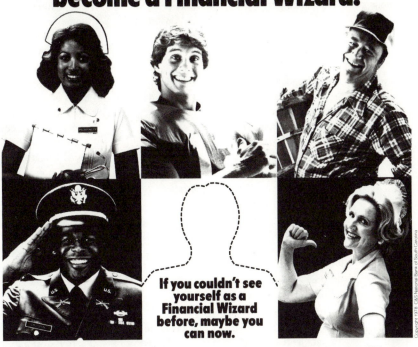

If you couldn't see yourself as a Financial Wizard before, maybe you can now.

We've been saying that "A lot of unlikely people are becoming Financial Wizards."

But maybe you consider yourself a little too unlikely.

Or maybe, just maybe, you're a little concerned about the idea of doing your banking with a machine instead of a person.

Well, there's no need to be nervous.

The machine won't kick, bite, scratch or foul up your account.

We don't claim that it's infallible. (It's only almost human, you know.)

But it's so easy to operate that even a child can learn to be a Financial Wizard. In one easy lesson.

Just insert your Financial Wizard card. Punch in your four-digit secret code.

Then follow the instructions on the TV screen. And you really can do almost all your banking, right then and there. Without having to go inside the bank.

All you have to do to become a Financial Wizard is open a C&S checking or savings account.

You'll find the only thing easier than becoming a Financial Wizard is actually making use of your new status as one.

Financial Wizards bank at C&S.
The Action Bank
The Citizens and Southern
National Bank of South Carolina

Financial Wizard's Media Schedule (first 10 weeks, when advertising was heaviest)

Media	Unit/Weights	Timing	Strategy/Rationale
Outdoor	50 showings.	4 weeks prior to ATM "on" date.	Teaser campaign: "Some very unlikely people will soon become Financial Wizards."
Newspaper	1/8 page ads (6 versions). Each ad weekly in daily and weekly newspapers.	4 weeks prior to ATM "on" date.	Teaser campaign: Photos of a demographic cross-section of people who would "soon become Financial Wizards."
	Full-page (2 versions). Each ad weekly for 6 weeks in statewide newspapers.	"On" date for 6 weeks.	Awareness: Emphasized ease of becoming a Financial Wizard.
Television	30-second spots. 350 GRPs/week in News, Prime Access, Prime, Late News, A.M. News.	"On" date for 6 weeks.	Awareness/impact: Designed to both announce the program and indicate ease of operation.
Radio	60-second, 2 spots in rotation. A.M./P.M. Drive, Weekdays, Sat./Sun. Drive, Afternoons, 200 GRPs/week.	Coincidental to TV for 6 weeks.	Same as TV: Aimed at active working populace.

The campaign broke in Columbia in August 1977 with "teaser" outdoor boards and newspaper ads indicating, "On September 1, some very unlikely people will become Financial Wizards." Follow up advertising—including TV, newspapers, and radio—solved the teaser and carried the campaign into 1978. (A media schedule is on the preceding page.) Support was complete, including bumper stickers, T-shirts, gifts, special editions of the bank's in-house newspaper, and a mobile demonstration van.

The campaign was rolled out across the state over the next 18 months at a cost exceeding $600,000.

Six months after the introduction, awareness of Financial Wizards was measured via random telephone survey. C&S was named first as the bank with ATMs by 57% of respondents; the next bank had awareness of 8%. It is important that 67% of respondents closely associated C&S with "Financial Wizards".

Thirteen months after the introduction, Financial Wizards were averaging 10,000 transactions per month per machine in Columbia and 9,000 transactions per month in Charleston—about double the original ambitious goal of 5000 transactions and nearly triple the 1978 national average of about 3500 transactions.

Bank management credits acceptance of ATM service by C&S customers as a major reason for the bank's ability to maintain low-cost checking and savings services for its large retail customer base, since the cost per transaction via ATM is less than that of a live teller transaction.

Equally important, new-account growth zoomed. Historically the number of new deposit and checking accounts opened had increased at a rate of 10% to 15% per year. In the year following the introduction of the Financial Wizards campaign, however, new accounts increased 80% faster than the previous year in Columbia, 70% faster in Charleston.

By 1984, C&S had 100 machines installed across South Carolina, with more planned.

MOM: C'Mon, son it won't bite you.

SON: Aw, mom, let's just go inside.

POLICEMAN: Hey, I was scared the first time too.

ANNOUNCER: A lot of unlikely people are becoming Financial Wizards at C&S. Some of them just need a little coaxing.

POLICEMAN: Look, this is how you make a deposit.

MOM: Naah. Show him how to make a loan payment.

ANNOUNCER: A Financial Wizard can do almost all his banking without going inside the bank -- any hour, any day. And all day -- and all night.

SON: Now I'll put it back into my savings account.

MOM: (LAUGHING) I think we've created a monster.

SON: Hey, this is kinda fun.

C&S Bank of South Carolina, "Nervous Wizard" (30 seconds)

What if no distinctive benefit can be discovered? Then the copywriter can use either or both of two techniques. One is known as "pre-emption," the other is "positioning."

Legend has it that "pre-emption" originated in the 1920s when a copywriter for a brewery was stuck in his search for a distinctive benefit. As part of his research, he toured the brewery and was amazed to learn that returned beer bottles were cleaned with steam before being re-used. He suggested that ads be created based on this theme, as showing how sanitary the brewery was. The advertiser demurred, noting that competitors cleaned their bottles with steam as well.

"That doesn't matter," said the copywriter. And he was right. Because the public associated the steam-cleaning of bottles with the copywriter's brewery, many chose to buy that beer.

The discount brokerage ad, discussed in Chapter 2, that offered Standard & Poor's research reports, which many competitors also supplied their customers, used "pre-emption," as does the Pittsburgh National Bank case history which follows. Featuring how comfortable the bank made applicants for loans feel drew prospects to Pittsburgh National's doors. The applicants didn't bother to think about whether other banks were equally courteous and hospitable.

NEWSPAPER PRE-PRINTS BOOST CONSUMER LOANS

Pittsburgh National Bank (PNB) wanted to increase the volume of its consumer loans, but PNB could not offer any points of superiority, such as lower interest rates, options, or quick evaluation of an applicant's credit. Consequently, PNB's agency, Ketchum Advertising/Pittsburgh, recommended pre-empting the position that "Pittsburgh National is the bank which helps consumers feel more comfortable during the loan application process."

The agency also recommended firmly establishing this position through the use of a newspaper insert consisting of four full pages placed three times during March and April in Pittsburgh's largest circulation newspaper, the Pittsburgh Press, and once or twice in a number of smaller newspapers. The inserts were supported by fractional-page newspaper ads, magazine advertising, and radio commercials on home improvement and education loans. One-hundred-seventy-five gross rating points a week of radio were bought for eight weeks in March, April, and May of 1984.

The front page of the insert consisted of two big headlines, "A Guide from Pittsburgh National Bank" and "How to Feel More Comfortable During the Uncomfortable Process of Getting a Loan." The second page featured a couple on a couch doing some figuring. The headline was "Know the unknowns." The copy stated that the best way to feel comfortable about getting a loan was to know in advance "what you should expect when you do come in and what your options are," followed by an explanation.

A guide from Pittsburgh National Bank.

How to feel more comfortable during the uncomfortable process of getting a loan.

When you meet with our loan officer, expect a pleasant surprise.

We know you wouldn't be applying for a loan unless you had a special need. And we also know coming into the bank may not be one of your favorite ways to spend time. So put yourself at ease. You're not going to be grilled.

What our loan officer will do is give you all the facts about our many types of loans. Because, in fact, there's more than one way to get the money you need.

We'll explain all our loans in as much detail as you want, including all the advantages and disadvantages. (See page 4

for a description of our various loans.) We'll work together to find the best loan for you. We'll help you with the paperwork. And we'll answer any questions you may have along the way.

You may not have to come in to apply. If you call your Pittsburgh National branch, you can apply over the phone and the papers will be mailed to you.

THE ANSWER TO WHY WE ASK ALL THOSE QUESTIONS.

First, we need to determine if you qualify for a loan. And, second, it's to help determine what kind of loan will be best for you.

You also may wonder why we ask what your loan is for. It's not that we want to pry. Fact is, the reason you want a loan has little bearing on the approval. You're the best one to decide if you need a loan.

If you have a once-a-year need (for example,

investing in an IRA or vacation), we may suggest an installment loan to be paid back in the next 12 months. (See chart on page 4.) But if you have an infrequent need (for example, remodeling your kitchen), we may suggest one of four different types of longer term loans.

Your answers to our questions will help us find the right loan at the best rate with payments that will fit your budget.

So when you come in to meet with your loan officer, expect to feel more comfortable than you ever imagined possible.

The third page showed a couple meeting with a loan officer and was headed "When you meet with our loan officer, expect a pleasant surprise." The copy explained how a loan officer helps and made clear that "You may not have to come in to apply. If you call your Pittsburgh National branch, you can apply over the phone and the papers will be mailed to you."

The back page was headed "Why you shouldn't choose a loan alone." The copy, lightened by spot illustrations, explained each of several subheads: Installment Loans, Government Guaranteed Education Loans, Turn Flexibility to Your Advantage, Visa/MasterCard, Check-Credit, Home Equity, Invest in Yourself, and Where to Go for Answers.

A 12-page four-color insert with magazine-size pages and the same copy was placed in TV *Guide* in June and in *Reader's Digest* in September.

The objective of this campaign was to increase consumer loan volume in the first six months of 1984 by 30% over the previous year's levels, while maintaining a high-quality loan portfolio. This objective was exceeded by 100%.

For a competitor to advertise the benefit once it's been pre-empted is inefficient. The competitor risks sounding like "me too." It's fighting for a tie instead of a win. And if the second bank's advertising is not highly distinctive, it will cause prospects to think of the first bank. This mistake is regularly made by companies that are not leaders in their industry. They copy the leader's advertising, but spend less than the leader, and so make the leader stronger.

"Positioning" is somewhat similar to pre-empting. In fact, pre-empting is sometimes considered a type of positioning. In its most obvious form, "positioning," consists of appealing not to every person in the audience but to a particular segment of the audience. The National Enterprise commercials (Chapter 7), for example, didn't appeal to everybody who might use the bank, but to professional people and owners of small businesses. Just stating the bank was for that group alone would cause many in that group to choose National Enterprise Bank.

The Citibank direct mail piece to police officers (Chapter 7) used positioning. Another example is the use of positioning by PaineWebber, described below.

HOW AN INVESTMENT BANK STIMULATED INTEREST IN ITS ABILITY TO ARRANGE MERGERS AND ACQUISITIONS

The problem facing PaineWebber Capital Markets Group in the early 1980s was this: Competing investment banks were arranging more and bigger mergers and acquisitions than PaineWebber. Furthermore, these competitors were continually advertising their activities, with both tombstones and image advertising.

The solution was arrived at by asking a number of questions. The key question turned out to be: Which client is to be preferred, the acquiring company or the acquired company? The answer was the acquired company. Yet no competing advertising appealed directly to this group! Competing advertising mostly bragged about the records the advertisers were establishing in number and size of mergers and acquisitions arranged.

The headlines and general thrust of the advertising proposed to PaineWebber by Benn & MacDonough, Inc., were based on a knowledge of the attitude of men and women who control companies that are suitable acquisitions. These owners or otherwise controlling persons don't like publicity, particularly for their business dealings. Thus the headlines and illustration in the ads shown. Note that the cartoon is not of the prospect but of someone the prospect wants to be disassociated from.

The advertisements, which appeared in different years, each received awards from the Financial Advertising and Marketing Association as outstanding institutional print ads. More important, when each ad appeared full-page in *The Wall Street Journal*, the merger and acquisition department's telephone rang continuously for days with responses of the kind the advertiser was pleased to receive.

132

USUALLY NOT THE WAY TO GET THE HIGHEST POSSIBLE PRICE

Sometimes putting a company or division on the auction block is necessary but more often, much more often, a quiet sale benefits both the seller and the buyer.

A quietly sold company or division is actually worth more than one everybody is gossiping about. Key executives have not left because of the uncertainty of their positions. Morale has not been damaged. And cooperation between managements after the sale is easier to obtain.

In arranging the quiet sale of a company or division, we have certain advantages. One is our ability to accurately evaluate a company. This derives partly from the large number of transactions in which we participate, partly from the acumen and experience of the people in our Merger & Acquisition Group, and partly from the research studies continually made by our affiliated brokerage companies, Paine Webber Mitchell Hutchins Inc. and Paine, Webber, Jackson & Curtis Incorporated. There's no industry in the U.S.A. that we don't know thoroughly.

Another advantage is our knowledge of so many potential buyers. We know them not just well, but very well —the kind of companies they want to acquire and the prices they are willing to pay.

They may be eager to buy your company or a division. If they can do so quietly.

For more information, call one of these direct lines to Managing Directors of our Merger & Acquisition Group:

Peter Slusser   (212) 730-4887
Jack Zinn   (212) 730-8722
Carole Lewis Anderson
  (212) 730-4827.

SOME RECENT QUIET ACQUISITIONS

In the past 6 years, our Merger & Acquisition Group has aided in the quiet sale, divestiture or acquisition of 187 companies and divisions, sometimes representing the seller, sometimes the buyer.

Most have been sold for from $5 million to $500 million in cash, securities or a combination. Typical recent sales in this range include Food Ingredient Businesses of Mal-linckrodt, Inc. to Carlin Foods Corporation for $40 million, Topaz, Inc. to Square D Company for $55 million, and the minority interest in Blue Chip Stamps to Berkshire Hathaway Inc. for $153 million.

Recent sales above $500 million include Dillon Companies, Inc. to The Kroger Co. for $650 million and Belco Petroleum Corporation to InterNorth, Inc. for $765 million.

PaineWebber
Incorporated

1221 Avenue of the Americas, New York, NY 10020 (212) 730-8500

In composing sentences and choosing words, the financial copywriter follows many of the principles that apply to other kinds of writing. The financial copywriter, however, has special problems because of finance's abstractness and the jargon so many professional people find handy in discussing finance. The skilled financial copywriter puts all the jargon into plain English that can be understood by anyone—which means that the copywriter needs to thoroughly understand what is being discussed in the first place.

More than in other kinds of writing, the financial copywriter usually finds it harder than other writers to arouse emotion in a way that will be acceptable to the advertiser, to prospects, and to the regulatory bodies. But that goes with the territory. The easy way out is to write ads that are only factual. Often they will be easily approved by the advertiser. But the most successful ads communicate some emotion. Every ad and commercial in this book does this—even when it appears to be only factual.

The experienced copywriter is continually on the alert, throughout the fact-gathering and parameter-determining process, to find ideas, words, and pictures that will hit a prospect's "hot-button"—that is, jolt a prospect into wanting the service being advertised.

The copywriter needs to so identify with the prospect that the copywriter can himself or herself feel the emotion that is to be engendered in the prospect.

There's no difference between the financial copywriter and other copywriters in this and many other respects. All types of copywriters need to know how to dramatize distinctive competitive differences, to pre-empt a benefit, and to appeal to a specific segment of the audience according to their occupation, position, wealth, attitudes, or other characteristics. The financial copywriter just faces a more formidable task.

WHICH LETTER TO PENSION PLANS FROM A CORPORATE BOND FUND PULLED THE MOST RESPONSES?

A few months after standards for investing pension fund money were established under the Employee Retirement Income Security Act (ERISA), the following two letters were mailed to alternate names on a list of 5000 moderate-sized pension funds.

Because the corporate bond fund preferred that its name not be used, the name of the fund has been reduced to "Income Fund, Series 2" and the salutation and letterhead have been omitted. The title below the signer's name was simply "Vice President." The sponsor's usual letterhead was used— name of firm, address, slogan, telephone numbers.

Because of the nature of the audience and the subject, the envelope and letter were kept as dignified as possible. There was no teaser on the envelope, no headline or summary box or P.S. in the letter. Key points in both letters were underlined, however.

The underlining of the paragraph beginning "For more complete information" was required by SEC regulations at the time.

To make it as easy as possible for respondents to answer, both letters were accompanied by a reply card headed in big type: "How fulfilling ERISA standards can be made easy while getting a current return of over 8%." To help the follow-up and improve the quality of the replies, respondents were asked to indicate the approximate net asset value of their fund.

Which letter pulled better is revealed on the page following the letters.

Dear Pension Plan Administrator:

Is the money in your company's pension plan being invested as well as it could be?

For example:

Is it growing at a rate of over 8% per year--consistently?

Can you tell how much the assets in your pension fund are worth without continual re-evaluation?

Is the administration easy, taking up little of your time?

Are your pension fund's investments liquid, so that you don't have any problems when cash is needed?

If your answer is "yes" to all of the above, read no further. If not, consider what the Income Fund, Series 2, has to offer:

* $8\frac{1}{4}$% per year current return. (This is the annual interest income after annual expenses, divided by the public offering price. It varies with either amount.)

* Your investment doesn't fluctuate in value and return the way common stocks do. The sizable and respected corporations which issued the under-lying bonds owe the interest and stated worth of the bonds. All of the bonds are "A" rated or better by one of the three established bond rating services.

* You receive a single certificate each time you invest. There are no coupons to clip. You do not have to watch to see if any bonds are called. You have no safe-keeping responsibilities.

* You can cash in units in amounts as small as $100 at any time, without any redemption charge.

* For more complete information about the Income Fund, Series 2, including charges and expenses, send for a prospectus by mailing the enclosed card. Read it carefully before you invest or send money.

Why delay? Mail the card today. If you prefer, telephone.

Dear Pension Plan Administrator:

May I send you, free and without obligation, a
brochure which tells about an easy way to fulfill
the ERISA requirements for your company's pension
plan?

It's a way that:

* obviously fulfills the prudent man and
  diversification requirements

* makes it unnecessary to re-evaluate your
  pension plan's assets every three years

* simplifies your annual report to the
  Department of Labor

* eliminates other administrative costs
  and dangers

* may reduce your company's contributions.

You get all these advantages--and more--when you
invest the capital of your company's pension plan in
the Income Fund.

Series 2 of the Income Fund consists of a diversified
portfolio of 23 bonds, not stocks. The bonds are all
"A" rated or better by one of the three bond rating
services.

The current return is 8¼%. This is the annual
interest income after annual expenses, divided by the
public offering price. It varies with either amount. You
get a relatively high fixed return without high risk.

For more complete information about the Income Fund
including charges and expenses, send for a prospectus by
mailing the enclosed card. Read it carefully before you
invest or send money.

Along with the prospectus, I'll also send you a
brochure which shows how the Income Fund can make it easy
for you to comply with ERISA requirements.

Why delay? Mail the card today, or if you prefer,
telephone.

THE BENEFIT TO THE PENSION PLAN OR THE BENEFIT TO THE ADMINISTRATOR?

The letter that stressed how the corporate bond fund could help the pension plan's investments pulled satisfactorily, but the letter that concentrated more strongly on how the brochure made it easy to fulfill ERISA requirements pulled three times as many responses. The more personal the benefit, the more effective it is likely to be. The agency was Benn & MacDonough, Inc.

10

HOW TO DESIGN AND ILLUSTRATE FINANCIAL ADVERTISING

Financial advertisements seldom win awards when competing with other kinds of advertising. In most award-winning competitions, the looks of the advertising count most, and only very occasionally do the parameters for a financial ad make illustrations the most effective design solution, as in the CIGNA ads.

Much of the time, those who design financial advertisements are stuck with headlines and copy that defy picturization. Forcing an inappropriate illustration on an ad can actually lower the responses. At one time in my career I believed that an illustration was essential, and I insisted that a certain ad include a metaphorical illustration. The ad pulled well enough in the advertiser's opinion, but not so well as I had anticipated. So we tried it again, eliminating the illustration, and the responses were much higher.

Picturing a potential prospect or even a booklet in the Bank of Boston gold ad would not have gained more responses of the quality desired at lower cost, I believe. The all-type advertisement set the correct tone for the subject (huge sums of money), the audience (multimillionaires living under uncertain political conditions), and the purpose (obtaining prospects who could readily be converted into customers).

The spot illustrations that appeared in some early Merrill Lynch ads were abandoned as not being worth their cost and trouble.

Adding an illustration would not have lowered the cost per response of either of the discount broker advertisements.

While most of the ads in this book include an illustration, most were produced under ideal conditions—that's one of the reasons they were so successful. In practice, the time between when the decision to advertise is made and when the ad must appear is sometimes too short for an illustration to be completed, and sometimes the budget or the space is too small.

141

When picturization is possible and desirable in financial advertising, the choice is often limited. Showing a checkbook in the Bank of America Investors Checking ad and the credit card in the Union Trust ad helped make these advertisements effective—were probably the best possible illustrations—but the ads cannot be termed beautiful, except to those who see the beauty in function rather than form.

Even when houses, automobiles, and yachts can be pictured, they must be symbolic. The house must stand for all houses, the automobile for all makes and styles, the yachts for all yachts that might be bought by prospects for the financial service. Consequently, picturing a house, car, or yacht in a uniquely intriguing way—which is how interest is fostered and how awards are won— often becomes anti-functional and would be counterproductive. For example, picturing a sleek Jaguar convertible driven by a beautiful girl, her blond hair streaming in the wind, would have reduced the number of auto loans California First Bank would have made, not increased them. Many prospects about to buy a Chevrolet sedan would have ignored the ad or been distracted from the benefit.

Yet the art director for financial advertising has one key advantage. He or she can depict people. Of all the various ways ads can be illustrated, those featuring people, on average, gain the most attention, particularly:

- those of people who are like the readers
- those of people who are showing emotion, as in the Financial Wizards ads
- those with a man and a woman together with some sexual connotations, as in the Nuveen "Sleep Nights" ad and the Chemical "Give Her the Kitchen She Deserves" ads
- those where the illustration is of real people, as in the Morgan Guaranty ads.

There's plenty of room for creativity in financial advertising. The truly creative art director need not be baffled by the abstract nature of finance, need not make the mistake of reducing the effectiveness of an advertisement in an attempt to make it different. He or she may not have a product to picture, but the most effective ads for tangible products often do not succeed simply by picturing the product, but by picturing the product *in use*—not a fur coat, but a woman enjoying the luxury of a fur coat, not a paper towel, but a paper towel wiping up efficiently. People are not motivated to purchase by the products themselves, but by the benefits the products confer on their owners. Financial ads can picture this—as in the Financial Wizards, "Sleep Nights," and "Give Her the Kitchen She Deserves" advertisements.

If the art director concentrates on what will make the advertisement most resultful, he or she can contribute much to the advertisement's success. Often these contributions will be unnoticed, yet they can make a significant difference.

Consider choice of type, for example. "Nobody buys a product because the advertisement was set in 10-point Garamond," David Ogilvy once said. Yet inappropriate type choices can cause fewer people to buy or to be affected as

intended. Setting an ad in a small, condensed typeface will lower the cost per response, because the ad will be smaller, but the image of the advertiser may suffer and readership may be reduced by those not immediately and strongly interested in the service at the time. The choice of typeface depends upon the ad's parameters and is up to the art director.

More often than in most other kinds of advertising, art directors in financial advertising are tempted to use several different sizes and faces of type. When making selections, the art director needs to use good taste and may find "Benn's Seven Degree Rule" useful in explaining to the less tasteful his or her choices. Benn's Seven Degree Rule applies to all art and derives its name from the problem of drawing two lines that may or may not be parallel. If the artist intends viewers to believe the two lines are parallel, they must be drawn at a 7 degree or greater angle to each other. If the angle is less, viewers will be unintentionally confused and the illustration will be less esthetic.

Similarly for music. It is the tone that is not distinctly different—that is just a little flat or sharp—that is unpleasant.

Similarly for color. Shades need to be sufficiently different so viewers instantly perceive that they are different.

And similarly for typefaces. When two or more are used, they need to be sufficiently different in size and/or style so they contrast to an extent immediately but unconsciously perceived by the reader.

A look at the ads in the successful case histories in this book may be useful not only for what they contain and for their style, but also for what they do not include. Illustrations are mostly photographs or realistic drawings. Realistic drawings are sometimes to be preferred because the quality of reproduction in some newspapers cannot be depended upon. And in any case, the photographs need to be very contrasty. Subtle shadings usually don't reproduce well.

Only two advertisements feature cartoons of people. Cartoons reproduce well even in the coarsest media, and nearly always attract attention and aid memorability.

The illustration in only one ad—"Sleep Nights"—is stylistic, and that needs to be so because it is metaphorical, because the style enhances its meaning, and because a photograph might have been deemed purient by some readers.

A bare majority of the illustrations feature the principal object connected with the service (booklet, credit card, what the borrowed money is to be used to purchase). Nearly as many feature people. Only one advertisement, that of the peanut for CIGNA, is neither an object connected with the service nor one or more persons.

Note that all the photographs are cropped rectangularly, or silhouetted, not in unusual shapes. There's nothing unusual about the type. And no logos are bigger than the headlines. In fact, most logos are modest in size, reinforcing the feeling that the advertiser puts the reader's interest first.

The creator of a television commercial faces problems similar to those of the designer of a print advertisement. Even more often than with print, showing

people gains the most attention and the greater returns at lower cost. People are more real in color and motion. They can be more empathetic. And they can inspire emotion, either by exhibiting it themselves or in other ways, more readily.

But sometimes other picturization will gain more attentive viewing and be more persuasive. The credit cards in the Union Trust commercial are an example.

And just as in print, some close judgments need to be made. For example, how much type should appear on the screen? It's well-established that showing words and saying them at the same time makes them more memorable. But supering words may make the commercial too hard-sell, may destroy the emotion that is being engendered.

Just as the judgments of the art director can make or break an advertisement, so the judgments of the creator (or creators) of a TV commercial regarding what will be pictured, and how, can make the commercial a great success or a dismal failure.

More than in other kinds of advertising, a financial ad or commercial needs to be like a windowpane. Usually the reader or viewer should be conscious not of the ad or commercial but only of the material or psychological benefits being offered. Only rarely should people think or say, "What an ad!" Instead they should think or say, "That's the financial service I want!"

The art director or creator of TV commercials who keeps that thought in mind may not win many awards in contests that do not consider the objective results obtained, but he or she will make more money for the advertiser, and him or herself.

11

HOW TO JUDGE
FINANCIAL ADVERTISING

Throughout this book, much has been made of what agencies contribute to the success of the advertising discussed, but the advertiser usually deserves most of the credit. The most successful advertising exploits a marketing advantage that is almost always developed by the advertiser. The California First advertising (in Chapter 3), for example, could not have been so successful if California First had not decided to lend money at rates lower than its competitors. The Financial Wizards advertising (in Chapter 9) featured a psychological advantage developed by the agency, but the advertising would not have been the success it was if customers could not do more with Citizen and Southern's ATMs than with those of competitors.

At the advertiser, it is the advertising director who usually deserves most of the credit. How well he or she defines the objectives and explains the parameters before any work is begun can make the difference between success, mediocrity, and failure. And he or she takes big risks. He or she must take responsibility for the advertising's success or lack thereof. If the advertising fails, the agency may lose one of its several clients. But the advertising director may lose his or her job—and have difficulty finding one just as good. And even when the advertising is successful, the advertising director must often field criticisms founded on faulty premises.

Further, the success of the advertising often depends upon the advertising director's ability to persuade others within the bank, investment firm, or insurance company of the advertising's appropriateness.

So, while many people must approve an ad or commercial before the advertising director—the copy director, art supervisor, creative director, management supervisor or other account person, review board—and while many may review the advertising within the advertiser's organization afterward, we'll discuss judging advertising from the viewpoint of the advertising director.

Theoretically, it's easy for an advertising director to judge advertising. He or she just needs to know the parameters and consider whether the advertising recommended by the agency fits. The advertising director can use his or her professional competence to judge how well recommended advertising will accomplish the purpose(s), will influence the target audience(s), suits the subject, utilizes the media, and will compete with similar services.

These parameters have been fully discussed in previous chapters and will only be summarized here in the form of checklists at the end of the chapter.

One parameter remains: the restrictions. The most obvious kind of restrictions consist of laws and regulations affecting the type of advertising being done. Each financial services industry—banking, investment, insurance—has its own set of laws and regulations. They are therefore discussed in separate chapters in Part Two of this book so readers can select the chapter(s) most pertinent to their needs.

The other kind of restrictions consist of the attitudes of the advertising director's bosses and colleagues.

"It always amazes me," said a friend of mine who sits on several boards of directors, "how everybody on a board considers himself an advertising expert. When we discuss other subjects—law, real estate, transportation, raising capital—the board members are modest and defer to specialists. But everybody thinks he can judge advertising."

Yet the bosses of a director of financial advertising are handicapped in several ways so far as judging advertising is concerned. In many other industries, the advertising director's boss once was the advertising director. This is seldom so in the financial services industry. Few top financial executives have experience or training in advertising, or have even read a book on the subject.

Like all businesspeople, most financial executives are not accustomed to thinking analytically about stimulating emotions with words and pictures. They are inclined to judge an advertisement as they do a painting, to judge a commercial as they do a movie. They either like it or they don't. They often appraise a proposed ad or commercial as if their own instinctive reactions were the same as those of the target audiences. But, of course, their backgrounds, viewpoints, and attitudes are quite different. In fact, while the differences between a target audience and the top managements in any industry are great, these differences are intensified in the financial services industry.

Financial executives are accustomed to thinking abstractly and in percentages and other numbers. Many are accustomed to making quick decisions, unemotionally, about huge sums of money. They know the details of the alternatives that a depositor, borrower, or investor can choose. And they have an informed opinion about how the relative advantages of those alternatives may shift in the future.

Prospects for financial services, in contrast, think concretely, more in terms of examples than abstractions. Many numbers usually confuse them. They prefer words. They're emotional about their money. Only seldom do they make decisions about huge sums, and then usually on inadequate knowledge. They usually have only a hazy, if any, idea about the alternatives to any action they may take regarding their finances. And their perceptions of possible changes in financial alternatives in the future are even more blurred.

In the real world the advertising director must be sensitive to discrepancies between the knowledge and attitudes of bosses and colleagues and those of the target audiences. Great advertising that never runs is wasted effort. Some advertising directors have survived by accurately guessing the kind of advertising their bosses like and judging the advertising recommended by the agency accordingly. Theirs is a precarious, nerve-racking existence. It succeeds when the bosses have unusually competent instincts regarding advertising, and/or when there is no objective measure of the advertising's success or lack of success, and/or when the advertising seems to make little difference in the profits of the advertiser.

Advertising directors for most mutual savings banks have needed to survive this way until recently because (1) mutual savings banks are owned by the depositors and there is no profit incentive and (2) only a few mutual savings banks objectively measured the results of their advertising.

But times are changing. Mutual savings banks are now fighting for their existence. All kinds of financial services organizations are becoming more professional in their marketing and advertising. Top managements increasingly want perceptible results from their advertising: telephone calls, letters, coupons, sales, visits to offices, a rising share of market, and increased awareness and improved attitudes as measured by surveys.

Only a naive, foolhardy or headstrong advertising director ignores the attitudes of his or her bosses and colleagues. But there is a considerable difference between being aware of these attitudes and basing one's judgment of advertising on them.

The truly professional advertising director considers all the other parameters and the legal and regulatory restrictions first when judging advertising recommended by the agency. If the advertising fits these parameters, then the director considers whether the boss(es) will readily approve it. If the boss(es) are likely to be reluctant, the advertising director considers how they can be persuaded to approve it.

If the boss(es) will take the time to listen to a long presentation, fine. If the boss(es) won't listen to much, a quick review of the character of the audience can often help to divert the boss(es) from thinking of the target audience as people like himself and move him toward making a sound decision.

Proposing that the advertising be tested by objective means, either before or after it has run, can often have a salutary affect on the judging. Just thinking about what the objective results may be forces executives to think objectively rather than subjectively.

Of course, the advertising director always needs to be careful in presenting advertising to allow for facts and policies which he or she doesn't know about. All knowledge is incomplete and uncertain. Top executives sometimes have reasons they can't communicate for disapproving proposed advertising.

Some advertising directors have found that unjustified sniping after the advertising has been approved can be mitigated by sending proofs to colleagues, sometimes with a rationale attached, so they can see in advance why their criticism would be foolish. And in any case, colleagues feel they have not been ignored.

But every situation is different. It is here that the advertising director's personal abilities in handling people comes into play.

In judging advertising recommended by the agency, a review of the case histories in this book may prove helpful—including what the ads and commercials do *not* feature.

None makes fun of the prospects. Never is the prospect portrayed except in a favorable light. Two cartoon ads in the previous chapter come close but (1) the PaineWebber cartoon depicts an executive of the kind from which prospects wish to disassociate themselves. (2) The Irving Trust cartoon and captions enhance the self-image of the prospects.

No print advertisement has a distracting pun in the headline. The "herd" in the Fidelity ad (in Chapter 8) might be considered a pun, but it's so apt that it doesn't detract, it reenforces the memory of the headline. The CIGNA commercial (in Chapter 1) features some puns, but they are used so skillfully that they do not distract and in fact are essential to the amusement. In addition, the principal purpose of the CIGNA commercials was to increase awareness. If their aim had been principally to gain conviction, the puns would have detracted from the purpose because of their double meaning, added confusion, and lack of straightforwardness.

In no ad or commercial do the jokes or other amusement overwhelm the point or points being made. In every case, the creativity fits the parameters snugly, is drawn from them, and is indivisible from the selling message. No entertainment idea that could apply to several different kinds of copy is included. There are no football pictures illustrating teamwork, no chess pieces with the headlines about the right move to make. None of the entertainment in the ads pictured could be applied to advertising with other parameters.

In no advertisement is the copy set in reverse. Art directors, desperate to make their advertising different, sometimes do this, but research shows that it reduces readership—as does printing over a tint or, worst of all, printing over an illustration. Headlines and copy in very large type may be okay in reverse or printed over an illustration, but they still are risky.

All the advertisements and commercials in the case histories in this book are distinctive. None promotes a competitor's brand.

Now, here are the checklists. Since, more than any other parameter, the purpose influences the overall characteristics of the advertising the most, there are two principal checklists—one for getting action and the other for improving image and increasing awareness. They are followed by supplementary questions that apply, regardless of the purpose, when the medium is television or radio.

CHECKLIST FOR JUDGING ADVERTISING THAT AIMS TO GET ACTION (Telephone Calls, Coupons, Letters, Personal Visits)

Whatever the Medium

Will the advertisement or commercial cause members of the target audience to want the benefit strongly enough to act as desired in large numbers? Will the significance of the benefit be easily comprehended by the most unsophisticated member of the target audience? If prospects are largely customers of a competitor, is the benefit, as communicated, sufficiently distinctive so as to attract them? If the principal purpose is to cause members of the target audience to visit the office, is the benefit made memorable? If customers or prospects are portrayed, will they like and identify with the way they are? If readers, viewers, or listeners are asked to telephone or visit an office, should and are the times to call or visit included? Is every effort made to make it as easy and convenient for readers, viewers, or listeners to respond? When feasible, is a reason given for readers, viewers, or listeners to act immediately, not to wait?

If the Medium Is a Newspaper or Magazine

Headline: Does the headline contain a strong benefit?
Illustration: Will inclusion of the illustration decrease or increase the cost per response? (The number of people attracted to the advertisement and impelled to act by the illustration may be fewer than the space and other costs connected with the illustration.) Would the illustration be equally or nearly as effective if it were smaller? (A large photograph may stimulate greater emotion, specifically desire, but it costs more.) Will the illustration have the effect desired? (An illustration of a booklet will increase the number of responses, but some who respond will be interested only in obtaining free information, not in the service being offered.) If the illustration is not a photograph, is there a good reason for its being a drawing or a cartoon? (Photographs, on average, gain the most attention. People are attracted and convinced by reality. But drawings and cartoons can be counted upon to reproduce well, may cost less, and can be more symbolic. They may even attract more attention and be more memorable, depending upon their style and content.) If the illustration is not a photograph, is it rectangular? (Odd

shapes detract from reality; on the other hand, silhouetting may help if the background would detract or be inconsequential.)

Copy: Will the copy increase the number of readers who will act as desired by: (1) reenforcing the benefit in the headline, (2) convincing readers that the advertiser can supply it, and (3) telling readers about additional benefits? If readers are asked to send money, is the copy long enough to stimulate sufficient desire among enough readers and to counter their objections? Is a coupon included? If not, why not? Valid reasons for not including a coupon are: (1) The principal purpose is to cause readers to visit the office. (2) An additional purpose is to increase awareness and improve image. (3) It is desired to reduce the number and improve the quality of responses. Overall, is every line, every phrase, every word worth the additional space it occupies? (That is, will it lower the cost per response?) If quality responses are desired, either easy-to-convert or upscale, should there be or are suitable screens included in the copy or coupon? Is there anything unclear, confusing, or otherwise distracting in the copy that will cause some readers to stop reading? (A direct response ad needs to be read all the way through to be effective.)

Type: If the headline is relatively long, is it in upper and lower case? (All-cap headlines are more difficult to read.) Could the body copy be smaller? (While 9-point with 1-point leading may be appropriate for most action-getting ads, 8- and even 7-point, may result in a lower cost per response.) Should the type be more condensed? Is the type easy to read? (Serif types are usually easier to read than sans serif, especially in the small sizes.)

Signature: Would reducing the size of the signature lower the cost per response? (If the purpose is solely to obtain telephone and coupon responses, no signature may be necessary, just the address in the coupon.)

If the Medium Is Direct Mail

Envelope: Is the address as personalized as it can be consonant with the cost of so doing? Is the name in the return address one which will deter recipients from opening the envelope? If so, can it be changed? Can a name be used which would encourage recipients to open the envelope? Does the envelope contain a teaser?

Enclosure: Is there more than one? (Usually the more the merrier—especially the order form or other response form should be separate, not a tear-off.) If a booklet is enclosed, is a covering letter enclosed as well? If not, why not? Does every enclosure contain a telephone number and/or address so, if a piece of the enclosure is separated from the order form, recipients can easily respond?

Letter: Does the letterhead help or hinder? Is the substance of the letter in a headline or box before the salutation? (This usually ups responses.) Otherwise, is the letter as much like a personal letter as possible? Does the beginning grab the reader's attention? Does the copy build desire? Are major objections countered? Are some objections better left unmentioned and not countered? (Some respondents may never have thought of them. The reminding, even though the objections are countered, may reduce rather than increase responses.) Is the letter signed in a colored ink? Does the title of the signer encourage respondents to reply? ("Sales Manager" or any similar title connoting sales reduces responses.) Does the letter contain a P.S.? (It can be the most powerful part of the letter because it is often read before the body of the letter and is then read again.)

Order Form: Does it contain a benefit, conspicuously displayed? Is it easy to understand? Does it contain a reason for acting immediately?

If the Medium Is Television

Is the commercial long enough to stimulate sufficient desire for the service? If viewers are asked to write and/or telephone, is enough time given to the address and/or telephone number? Are the address and/or telephone number both shown and told? Are they repeated in the audio? If viewers are asked to visit an office, is the benefit strong enough and well-linked to the advertiser?

CHECKLIST FOR JUDGING ADVERTISING THAT AIMS TO CHANGE ATTITUDE AND INCREASE AWARENESS

Whatever the Medium

Is the advertiser made memorable in a favorable way? Is the advertiser made distinctly different from competitors by a unique benefit, preemption, position, or other means? Will the entire advertisement or commercial, considering its size or length, form, and content, cause: (1) prospective customers to feel that the advertiser is an organization they would like to do business with, (2) prospective employees to feel that this is a company they would like to work for, and (3) opinion-makers to feel that this is an organization they would gladly recommend to prospective customers and employees?

If the Medium Is Print

Illustration and Headline: Will the attention of all the target audiences be attracted? Will readers who look only at the illustration, headline, and signature be favorably influenced? (About seven times as many people will look only at the illustration, headline, and signature as will read the copy.) Is the illustration a rectangular photograph? Why not?

Headline and Copy: Does the headline contain a benefit and/or news and/or entertainment—or indicate that a benefit and/or news and/or entertainment is contained in the copy? Do the headline and/or copy just brag, or do they tell, or at least imply, that the advertiser helps or can help the target audience(s) and/or society in general? Is the copy convincing? Is the copy set in type large enough to make reading easy by the most casual reader?

Signature: Is the name of the advertiser big enough so that it will readily be seen by casual readers? Is it small enough so that it will be seen after, but not before, the illustration and headline? Is its style consistent with the financial organization's signage and letterheads?

If the Medium Is Television

Is the advertiser's name repeated often? Is the advertiser's name both told and shown?

ADDITIONAL QUESTIONS TO ASK IF THE MEDIUM IS TELEVISION OR RADIO

Will the beginning prevent members of the target audience from switching channels, engaging in conversation, or leaving the room? Is the message simple and easily comprehended? Will the body of the commercial hold attention and increase the interest of the target audience?

If the medium is television: (1) Does the commercial make full use of television's potentialities—action, color, movement of the camera, and sequence of scenes? (There may be a good reason not to, but it must be deliberate.) (2) Is the heart of the message shown, not just told?

PART II:
HOW REGULATIONS AFFECT FINANCIAL ADVERTISING

If an advertisement includes a picture of U.S. currency, the reproduction cannot be in color and must be either 25% smaller than the actual money or 50% larger. That's about the only regulation that applies to more than one of the three kinds of financial advertising—bank, investment, and insurance. Each kind has its own set of regulations and regulators.

Bank advertising is regulated mostly by the Federal Deposit Insurance Act, the Federal Reserve Act, the Consumer Credit Protection Act, and regulations promulgated by the Federal Deposit Insurance Corporation (FDIC), the Federal Savings & Loan Insurance Corporation, the Governors of the Federal Reserve System, the Comptroller of the Currency, and the Federal Trade Commission.

Investment advertising is regulated mostly by the Securities Act of 1933, the Investment Company Act of 1940, and the regulations promulgated by the Securities and Exchange Commission, the National Association of Securities Dealers, the New York Stock Exchange, and other exchanges.

Insurance advertising is free from federal regulation. Each of the 50 states has its own set of regulations. They have much in common, however.

The next three chapters analyze only the most pertinent regulations—and do so in language that may make some lawyers shudder. General statements are made for which there are exceptions. Everyday words are often substituted for more precise legal terms. And sometimes what *can* be done (rather than what *cannot* be done) is stated—which is often legally difficult.

The purposes of this discussion are to help writers create more effective financial advertisements and to help those who must judge ads and commercials decide whether any regulations are being blatantly flouted.

In many financial organizations, an executive outside the advertising chain-of-command, often trained as a lawyer, keeps up with the regulations and decisions under the regulations. This person approves or disapproves proposed advertising, making it possible for creative people to apply their thinking freely as to what is objectionable and what is not. If they are wrong, they can always go back to the drawing board, or perhaps just make a slight modification that will enable the advertising or commercial to pass.

For example, early in my career lawyers objected to the way I had described the use of commodity futures contracts. I had stated that an investor who enters into a contract to buy a commodity, such as wheat, at some stated time in the future does not intend to accept delivery of the wheat. Before the date the wheat is due, he or she intends to enter into an offsetting contract to sell the wheat before the delivery date stated in the contract. The lawyers agreed that this was true, but also said this couldn't be stated because it meant that the investor was intending to violate a contract. From my point of view, this statement was fundamental to communicating an understanding of the use of commodity contracts. Eliminating the statement would have made everything else I had written incomprehensible. After some thought, and in desperation, I asked, "Could it be changed to read that most investors actually do not accept delivery but enter into an offsetting contract?" They immediately agreed. A small change made the statement permissible, but the creative person, not the person in charge of compliance, made the suggestion—which is the usual and correct allocation of responsibilities.

The more advertising people know about the regulations and how they can be met, the better, yet one question can serve as a guide to both beginners and experienced creators and judges of financial advertising: Is the advertising false or misleading, in part or as a whole? If the answer is yes the ad is illegal, regardless of what specific regulations state. Preventing financial advertising from being misleading, particularly to the unsophisticated, is the principal purpose of the regulations.

12

BANK ADVERTISING REGULATIONS

Most of the regulations affecting bank advertising concern interest rates on deposits and loans, the use of endorsements, and inclusion of "Member FDIC," "Member FSLIC," or a similar statement in an ad.

INTEREST RATES

The key provision is that interest rates must be stated as simple interest for a 12-month period. The actual interest that depositors receive or borrowers pay may be higher because of compounding, but the interest must be stated as if there were no compounding.

This rule doesn't prevent stating the percentage that results from compounding during the year, but the annual interest rate must be given equal prominence. (See the Bank of America ad in Chapter 1.)

Further, no advertisement may show the percentage return based on more than a year. This applies not only to regular deposits but to money market certificates as well. (See the CrossLand Savings ad on the following page.)

Peculiarly enough, however, banks seem to be allowed to make general statements that a depositor's money will double or triple within so many years at the stated amount of interest. Maybe this is to allow banks to compete with investment firms that can make similar statements about an investment in certain debt securities, such as CATS (Certificates of Accrual on Treasuries).

In order to prevent any bank advertisement from misleading readers, viewers, or listeners, several regulations affect ads featuring interest rates that are earned only under certain conditions. If a minimum amount must be deposited or the money must be left on deposit for a certain period of time, these facts must be clearly and conspicuously stated. If a deposit earns a lower rate because it is

How CrossLand makes your money work.

	ANNUAL RATE*	ANNUAL YIELD
36 Month Account	**9.75%**	**10.24%**
30 Month Account	**9.75%**	**10.24%**
24 Month Account	**9.50%**	**9.96%**
12 Month Account	**9.25%**	**9.69%**
6 Month Account	**8.75%**	**9.14%**
90 Day Account	**8.40%**	**8.76%**

*$500 minimum deposit. Compounded daily, credited monthly. No additional deposits allowed. Federal regulations require substantial penalty for premature withdrawal.

Liquid Investment Account℠

8.49%
effective annual yield on
8.15%
annual rate on maintained deposit of $50,000 or more.

8.33%
effective annual yield on
8.00%
annual rate on maintained deposit of $2,500 to $49,999.99.

Compounded daily, credited monthly. Rate guaranteed for 30 days. Offering rates subject to change.

CrossLand Savings

Keep in touch where your money works

Offices located in Manhattan, Brooklyn, Queens, Staten Island, Nassau, Westchester and Rockland Counties and affiliates Coast to Coast.

Rates apply to New York offices only.

SM–Liquid Investment Account is a Service Mark of CrossLand Savings FSB.

Member FDIC   Assets Over $8 Billion

Savings bank advertisement created and placed by Vitale Advertising Inc. (actual size). Note that the rate and yield are of equal type size and that the comparisons are all for one year. Note too the mandatory statements throughout the ad.

withdrawn in fewer years than required to earn the stated rate, that fact must be stated with equal prominence along with the lower rate.

It's not enough to say that a rate is "guaranteed" for a specified number of years. Language must be used that plainly indicates that a depositor must commit money for a certain length of time in order to earn the advertised rate. It is particularly objectionable to state that a rate is earned on money "held," "kept," or "left" on deposit for a specified number of years, as this suggests that a depositor can withdraw the funds at any time. Similarly, it is also not sufficient just to use statements such as "5 1/2% for 90 days" or "6% for 1 year."

Further, advertisements featuring time deposits must include the statement "Substantial interest penalty is required for early withdrawal" or some similar statement.

Certificates of deposit may be given other names, such as "savings certificate" or "savings bond," but language must then be included that makes it clear that it is not a savings account in the usual sense and that withdrawals are restricted.

All comparisons made with other rates must be fair and not subject to misinterpretation, particularly not misinterpretation in favor of the advertiser. For example, an advertisement cannot compare the rate on an account at the advertiser's bank that requires that money be kept on deposit for two years with the rate that another bank pays on its regular savings accounts without making the difference in the accounts abundantly clear.

The rate on a Treasury bill is a *discount* rate which is numerically lower than if it were stated in terms of return, as is usual for bank deposits. The advertiser must either make this clear or state the effective yield on a six-month Treasury bill on a comparable basis.

Some special regulations apply to advertising certificates of deposit maturing in 26 weeks. Such advertising must contain the sentence "This is an annual rate and is subject to change at renewal." This statement helps to avoid any misunderstanding on the part of a depositor that the rate applies for a year—an easy misunderstanding since the return is stated as an annual rate of return but only applies for the six months.

The interest rates that banks pay on 26-week certificates of deposit continually change, so care must be taken that an advertisement does not offer a rate that is no longer obtainable. If an ad must be placed too far in advance to be current or will be displayed for several weeks, a rate may be advertised without misunderstanding by using phraseology such as "Had you bought this bank's six-month money market certificate on Wednesday, November 6, 1985, you would be receiving 8.75% interest."

Further, if the return on a six-month certificate of deposit is based on the rate of six-month Treasury bills, then the copy must state clearly and conspicuously that Federal regulations prohibit compounding of interest on Treasury bills during the term of the deposit.

The rules for loans are similar to those for deposits. The interest that the borrower must pay on the loan must be an annual percentage rate. (See the Bank of California ad in Chapter 3.)

Further, the borrower cannot be given partial information about the terms of the loan so as to make it seem more appealing. If an advertisement states any of the following—

• The dollar amount of interest that must be paid on the loan
• The number of installments
• The period of repayment
• The amount of the down payment, if any

then the ad must also include the terms of repayment and the down payment, if any, besides, of course, the annual rate of interest that must be paid on the loan.

Basically what all this means is: Don't try to attract deposits or loan business by fooling around with the interest rate. It's not only unethical, but it will get you in trouble with the authorities. There are better ways, as shown in this book. Much better to enhance the benefit of the interest rate with words, as in the first case history in this book. Regulations prohibit the use of only one word. "The term 'profit' shall not be used in referring to interest paid on deposits," say the regulations.

ENDORSEMENTS

Banks are lucky so far as endorsements are concerned. Unlike investment firms, bank advertisements featuring endorsements need meet only the same requirements as those of general ads. The only regulator is the Federal Trade Commission. The key rules are:

• Endorsements must always reflect the honest opinions, findings, beliefs, or experience of the endorser. Further, the advertisement cannot be used if the endorser stops being a customer of the bank.
• The endorser can't say anything that the bank can't back up. If the endorser makes a wild claim that the bank can't substantiate, the bank is in violation of FTC rules.
• If models or actors are used in photographs or on TV in pseudo-endorsements and they are not customers, the fact that they are not must be clear, either by implication or by stating so clearly.

"MEMBER FDIC"

The regulations state that all members of the Federal Deposit Insurance Corporation (FDIC) or the Federal Savings & Loan Insurance Corporation (FSLIC) need to include a statement to that effect in all advertisements and commercials that mention deposits, whenever feasible.

The statement does not need to be included in ads and commercials that only concern loans, safe deposit boxes, trust services, real estate, armored car services, analyst or service charges, securities, travel, and bank life insurance.

Some other exceptions are common sense. The statement does not need to be included in radio and television commercials of 30 seconds or less, unless a TV commercial merely displays the bank's name. Other exceptions include:

- A joint ad by several banks, some insured, some not
- Ads of statements of condition required by law
- Ads where including the statement is obviously impractical, such as on pens, pencils and key chains.

The "the" and/or the words "of the" may be omitted from the standard phrase "Member of the Federal Deposit Insurance Corporation." In fact, the phrase may be reduced to "Member of FDIC" or even to "Member FDIC." (See the 60-second Bank of America radio commercial in Chapter 1.) Even further, if the official symbol used is very small, it may consist only of the initials FDIC in the official type-style. The symbol consists of FDIC in big block letters with the FDIC seal within the "C." Over the letters FDIC in smaller type are the words "Each depositor insured to $100,000." Below are the words "Federal Deposit Insurance Corporation."

The same regulations apply to "Member of the Federal Savings & Loan Insurance Corporation."

Since the statement or complete symbol is obviously a benefit to customers doing business with the bank, and since the exceptions are permissive, not mandatory, it makes sense to include the statement or symbol in just about any print advertisement of a member bank.

Most banks are members of the FDIC or the FSLIC. Only state chartered banks may not be, and this may be changed.

To sum up bank advertising regulations: The rate for a deposit or loan must be in simple annual interest. It's a good idea to show the actual yield on deposits for the year as well as the annual interest, as most banks do. It's necessary to make sure that the information about the conditions applying to the deposit or loan cannot be misunderstood. Include the complete insured savings logo whenever feasible. If not, at least include "Member FDIC" or Member FSLIC."

13

INVESTMENT ADVERTISING REGULATIONS

Many people concerned with investment advertising have completed their entire careers without knowing much about tombstone advertising—that is, announcements of public offerings of securities. Yet our discussion will begin with the laws and regulations affecting tombstone advertising—and then go on to discuss mutual fund advertising and other kinds of investment advertising—for two reasons:

1. Those who create and judge other kinds of investment advertising, especially mutual fund advertising, will find it easier to understand what can and cannot appear in investment advertising of any kind.

2. Increasingly, agencies with no experience in tombstone advertising are finding it necessary and/or profitable to enter this field. For decades prior to 1967, only two agencies—Albert Frank–Guenther Law and Doremus & Company—were competent to place tombstone advertising. Other agencies currently competent in this field, such as Benn & MacDonough, became competent only by employing people who had tombstone experience at Albert Frank or Doremus. We shall see why this is so.

TOMBSTONES

The laws and rules that govern the contents of tombstone advertising were enacted to correct abuses that took place in the 1920s. One of the apparent objectives of those laws and rules was to insure that anyone making a decision about whether to buy a stock (or other widely distributed security) would receive all the pertinent available information about the security and the issuing company.

The effect, in practice, may not be what was originally intended, but it is far preferable to what went on in the 1920s, when new issues were often sold on skimpy information and unsubstantiated promises.

Section 5 of the Securities Act of 1933 makes it mandatory that, with certain exceptions, solicited buyers of publicly offered securities receive a prospectus—that is, a booklet—containing *full* information about the company and the securities being offered. They can't be given *partial* information in writing about what a great buy a security is. On the other hand, the final prospectus can't be printed until the price of the stock or other security is established. And once the price is established, it's necessary that the issue be sold out quickly. How much investors are willing to pay for a security is continually changing.

As a consequence, the real selling of a publicly offered issue is done orally—almost entirely by telephone. The buyers receive a prospectus after they have unofficially agreed to buy. The prospectus requirement does, however, restrain those selling publicly offered securities to oral statements that can be backed up by the prospectus. And it limits most advertising to announcing the fact that the offering has been made—to tombstones.

The process leading up to the placement of a tombstone ad usually begins

---

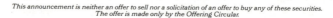

This announcement is neither an offer to sell nor a solicitation of an offer to buy any of these securities. The offer is made only by the Offering Circular.

September 4, 1985

525,000 Shares

 SUFFIELD SAVINGS BANK

Common Stock

Price $18.00 Per Share

Copies of the Offering Circular may be obtained in any State from only such of the undersigned as may legally offer these securities in compliance with the securities laws of such State.

Advest, Inc.

Bear, Stearns & Co.	The First Boston Corporation	Alex. Brown & Sons Incorporated	Drexel Burnham Lambert Incorporated
Goldman, Sachs & Co.	Kidder, Peabody & Co. Incorporated	Merrill Lynch Capital Markets	Morgan Stanley & Co. Incorporated
PaineWebber Incorporated	Prudential-Bache Securities	Salomon Brothers Inc	Shearson Lehman Brothers Inc.
Smith Barney, Harris Upham & Co. Incorporated	Thomson McKinnon Securities Inc.		Dean Witter Reynolds Inc.
A. G. Edwards & Sons, Inc.		Moseley, Hallgarten, Estabrook & Weeden Inc.	
Tucker, Anthony & R. L. Day, Inc.	Burgess & Leith Incorporated	Coburn & Meredith, Inc.	Fahnestock & Co. Inc.
First Albany Corporation	Gruntal & Co., Incorporated	Herzfeld & Stern Inc.	Janney Montgomery Scott Inc.

weeks before, with the advertising agency being notified that a public offering of securities is being registered with the Securities and Exchange Commission by the agency's client, the managing underwriter. The agency usually writes and distributes a news release to this effect immediately.

The registration statement contains fulsome information about the securities being offered and the issuing company. With certain technical sections deleted, it becomes the prospectus that is ultimately delivered to buyers of the securities.

Over the next several days or weeks, members of the staff of the Securities and Exchange Commission (SEC) review the registration statement and may require that it be amended. Or it may be amended at the initiation of the underwriter for one reason or another.

During this period, members of the underwriting group talk to investors and dealers to see whether and to what extent they would be interested in buying the shares, either for themselves or on behalf of their customers. Technically, orders cannot be taken, only "indications of interest."

When the SEC approves the registration statement, an advertisement is placed as promptly as possible in one or more publications. Only under extraordinary conditions is TV or radio used. The ad has been prepared in advance by the agency, awaiting the day and hour when the registration statement "becomes effective."

To enable the agency to prepare the announcement, the managing underwriter gave the agency a "red herring"—that is, a preliminary prospectus based on the registration statement sent to the SEC but not yet approved—plus a list of the members of the underwriting group and the dollar amounts of the securities that each underwriter has committed itself to sell.

The agency recommends the size of the advertisement, which depends mostly upon the dollar amount of the underwriting. The agency also suggests the media in which the advertising might appear. Most new-issue advertising appears only in the *Wall Street Journal*, but some ads are placed in other publications as well, principally *The New York Times, Barron's, Forbes, Fortune, BusinessWeek*, and *Investment Dealers Digest*. The ad may also be placed in specialized financial publications and trade publications appropriate to the nature of the security (such as *The Market Chronicle, The Bond Buyer, The Fixed Income Journal*) or the nature of the company. An offering by a microchip manufacturer might be placed in *Electronics*, for example.

Agencies cannot present a media plan with the same forceful, logical reasoning with which the best of them back up most of their media recommendations, because the reason(s) for placing the advertising are ill-defined and often unrecognized. In most instances the advertising does not help sell the issue. It has already been sold through the "indications of interest" obtained prior to the appearance of the advertising. In fact, in most instances the issue has been entirely sold out before the ad appears. Underwriters make every effort to confirm the indications of interest—that is, to legally sell the issue—the day the registration statement becomes effective. Often this is accomplished in hours. And the ad cannot physically appear until the next day because there's always a chance that the registration will not be approved on the date anticipated. Further, with common stock and some debt offerings, the price at which the securities will be offered is not known until the effective date.

Most tombstone advertising has, or may have, any or all of four functions.

1. *A tombstone enhances the image of those investment firms appearing in the advertisement*, especially the image of the managing underwriter. A member of the underwriting group may benefit by having the name of the firm seen by (a) chief executive and financial officers who will be impressed and so be more likely to discuss any contemplated financing with the firm, and (b) other underwriters, who will be managing an underwriting in the future, who seeing the firm in the tombstone may be influenced to include the firm in the underwritings they manage.

As far back as 1874, co-managers of a proposed underwriting of U.S. government bonds were concerned about the prestige conferred by a tombstone advertisement. The House of Rothschild, then the greatest private bank in the world, did not want to include the name of the co-manager. Eventually, in order to be included, J. & W. Seligman & Co. accepted a smaller share of the underwriting—28% instead of the originally agreed upon 37 1/2%. The prestige of appearing in the tombstone was worth more than a bigger profit.

2. *Tombstone advertising usually pleases officers of the company whose issue is being underwritten* (and it is the company whose security is being underwritten that pays for the advertising, which is included in the underwriters' bill). The officers may like seeing the issue advertised, to some extent out of vanity, but mostly because the advertising may improve the regard with which the company is held by security analysts, institutions, and other investors. Capital is normally raised for expansion. And a growing company is usually an attractive investment.

3. *Tombstone advertising may support the price of the security in the days after the offering.* It may attract buying from investors who did not know about the offering in advance because they were not contacted by underwriters and dealers. It may also spur buying among investors who were contacted but who were undecided.

Both the underwriters and the company whose security was underwritten benefit if the price of the security goes up in the days following the public offering. Those who bought the security are pleased and are likely to remain active customers of the underwriter. The company will find it easier to raise capital in the future. And company officers may themselves own large amounts of the common stock or other offered security.

4. *Tombstone advertising may stimulate buying and therefore help underwriters and dealers sell the securities* (a) on those rare occasions when the issue is not sold out the same day and (b) when the underwriters feel that placing the advertisement in advance of the effective date is necessary to help sell the issue. This can be done by inserting a long paragraph in the tombstone stating that the registration statement has not yet become effective and placing it in advance of the offering.

Whatever the purpose of a specific tombstone, the procedure for preparing the advertisement is usually the same. In arranging the names of the underwriters in the ad, the agency divides them into categories, called "brackets," by the size of commitment. Those underwriting the most are in the top bracket, those underwriting the next most are in the second bracket, and so on. The underwriters are listed alphabetically within brackets, so by examining the ad knowledgeable people can easily figure out which bracket an underwriter is in—just by noting when the alphabetical order begins all over again.

In the tombstone for Suffield Savings Bank, shown earlier in this chapter, placed by Benn & MacDonough, new brackets begin with A. G. Edwards & Sons and Burgess & Leith. And the underwriters in the Burgess & Leith bracket appeared only in the Eastern edition of *The Wall Street Journal*; other underwriters appeared in this space in other editions.

Different versions of the advertisement may be prepared for each edition and printing of *The Wall Street Journal*. *The Wall Street Journal* is printed in five editions: Eastern, Midwestern, Southwestern, Western, and International. And most editions are printed at more than one location. Usually underwriters in lower brackets are included only in those editions or printings of *The Wall Street Journal* where they are headquartered. The advertising agency makes these decisions, subject to the approval of the managing underwriter, based on the agency's records.

The agency needs to know much more than where each underwriter is headquartered. Of great importance, as you can imagine, is getting the name of each underwriter precisely the way the underwriter wants it to appear in the advertisement. The agency does not receive the names from the managing underwriter in full, but only enough of the name sufficient for identification: "First Boston" not "The First Boston Corporation," and "Donaldson Lufkin" not "Donaldson, Lufkin & Jenrette Securities Corporation." The agency also needs to know many other details, such as whether "Incorporated" should follow or be under the rest of the firm's name, whether it is abbreviated, and even if the "Inc." is followed by a period or not.

And since firms are continually merging, being acquired, being formed, and changing their names or their preferences, the agency must keep up-to-date on these matters.

The agency also needs to know which legal language should be used in which ads. Only in unusual circumstances, or for a new form of securities, does the agency ask the managing underwriter, who has more pressing matters to attend to during these critical hours, for this information.

Essentially, a tombstone identifies the security being offered, states the price, and lists the underwriters from whom a prospectus may be obtained. It may also state (but it is not required): whether the securities are a new issue, and/or the address(es) of firms from whom a prospectus can be obtained.

Most tombstones contain all this information, except the address(es), plus the approximate date of the offering and the necessary legal phraseology.

The additional information is limited to:

- The yield and the rating(s) of bonds and other debt securities
- Whether income from the security is tax-exempt
- Details about a rights offering
- Whether the security is a legal offering for savings banks, insurance companies, and similar investors
- Any phraseology a state or other authority may require
- A brief indication of the type of business the issuer is in.

Manufacturers, utilities, and similar companies seldom take advantage of this last item, but mutual funds and similar issuers do. In fact, it is this loophole that allows mutual funds to place ads that do not look like tombstones (yet legally are) and that are far more effective. More about this in our discussion of mutual fund and unit investment trust advertising.

MUTUAL FUNDS

Writing or judging a direct response advertisement for a mutual fund or similar investment vehicle requires a greater knowledge of regulations than for any other investment service. Mutual funds continually offer their shares to the public, so the rules for tombstone advertising usually but not always apply. Mutual fund advertising is affected by additional rules under the Securities Act of 1933 as well as by the Investment Company Act of 1940, which defines mutual funds and similar investment vehicles.

"Mutual fund" is a term invented by investment marketing people for the type of investment legally known as an "open-end management investment company."

"Management" means that securities owned by the company are bought and sold with the objective of improving the asset value or income of the company. The "open-end" means that sales are continually being offered to the public in order to increase the company's capital and/or replenish capital that has been depleted by some investors redeeming their shares.

A "closed-end management investment company" is one that does not continually offer its shares to the public. Generally it has been formed by a one-time offering of shares. Further, a closed-end investment company does not stand ready to redeem its shares at any time, as is usual with an open-end company. Consequently, tombstone advertising rules do not apply to advertising by closed-end investment companies except at the time of their formation. But a closed-end investment company has much less incentive to advertise. It does not need to continually replenish its capital because of redemptions. If an investor wishes to sell (or buy) shares in a closed-end investment company, he or she sells (or buys) through his or her broker, just as he or she would sell or buy any stock, such as General Motors common.

When first promulgated, the principal rule governing tombstone advertising,

Rule 134, confined mutual funds to tombstones just like those for industrial companies. Later it was expanded, partly because officials of the SEC came to realize that the rigidity of the regulation harmed investors more than it helped them, partly because the industry had changed, and partly to codify and control devices developed by ingenious advertising people.

Originally the language stating how an investment company could identify itself in advertising was as follows: " . . . whether it is a balanced, specialized, bond, preferred stock or common stock fund, or whether in the selection of investments emphasis is placed on income or growth characteristics. . . . "

It was similar to the permission allowed for describing industrial companies.

The original language in Rule 134, as you can see, allowed open-end investment companies, which quickly came to be called mutual funds, to include investment objectives in their advertising. And since the objective, if attained, is the benefit to investors, mutual fund advertising soon abandoned the traditional tombstone format and adopted that of the traditional direct response advertisement. The headline contained the benefit (the objective); the body copy contained more information, related sometimes tenuously to the objective; and a coupon was used to happily conform to the requirement that investors be informed of where they could get a prospectus.

Rule 134 originally said nothing about any illustration, so advertising people, in an effort to get some emotion into mutual funds ads, started to include illustrations, such as the Dreyfus lion. They had some precedent on their side, as tombstones for industrial and similar companies were increasingly featuring the company's logo. But the SEC balked. The people there wanted to keep emotion out of the ads. After much shifting back and forth, eventually the current regulation was adopted: Any illustration may be included if it is appropriate for inclusion in the company's prospectus (whatever that means).

As more and more information came to be included in mutual fund advertising, regulators felt that potential investors needed to be advised there was much more to know, especially that investors needed to know that a management fee and sometimes a sales charge was involved. Further, since the ads were getting to be so effective, investors needed to be warned that they shouldn't send in money but should wait until they had read a prospectus first. Hence the current rule that every mutual fund ad with selling copy include the following sentence:

"For more complete information about (Name of Company) including charges and expenses (get) (obtain) (send for) a prospectus from (Name and Address) (by sending this coupon). Read it carefully before you invest or (pay) (forward funds) (send money)."

Purists are not allowed to correct the fuzzy English of the SEC. "More complete" violates the meaning of "complete," but the phrase can be excused because it accomplishes the SEC's intent.

If an advertisement does little more than identify the mutual fund and contain the fund's objective, the "For more complete information . . . " legend need not be included.

However, a mutual fund advertisement that does contain the legend may include information in addition to that allowed in any tombstone for a public offering. This additional information must conform to either of two SEC rules, which cannot be mixed together. An ad conforms to either Rule 134 or Rule 482.

Under Rule 134, a mutual fund advertisement containing the legend may include any or all of the following additional information:

- The kind of securities in which the fund invests (common stocks, preferred stocks, bonds, convertible securities, options, or a combination or a specialized type)
- The objective (income or growth or hedge against inflation or a combination)
- Goals such as retirement
- The name of the mutual fund's advisor (most funds retain a separate company that decides what securities shall be bought and sold and when; actually, the advisor usually creates the investment company)
- The corporate symbol
- An attention-getting headline that does not contain performance figures and that does not violate any of the other regulations
- An attention-getting illustration appropriate for inclusion in the prospectus
- Policies, services, and method of operation
- Principal officers
- When or for how long the fund or its advisors have been in existence
- Total value of the investment company assets managed by the fund's advisor
- A discussion of economic conditions
- The fact that it is a mutual fund

Note that while objectives and goals may be stated, describing how well the fund has met an objective or goal is forbidden, as is implying that the investment objective will be achieved.

Rule 482, sometimes referred to as "the omitting prospectus rule," was promulgated originally in 1979 and amended in 1983. It allows a mutual fund ad to include any information that is in the prospectus. However, the ad can *only* include information, the substance of which is in the prospectus. This rule allows, for example, performance figures to be used in a mutual fund ad so long as the prospectus contains that information. Suppose, however, the copywriter or the advertising manager wants to discuss inflation or some other economic condition, facts about which are not included in the prospectus. Or suppose it is desired to make some comparisons with other kinds of investments. Neither can be done under this rule, but could be included under a Rule 134 ad if appropriately worded.

When an advertisement tells how much the shares of a mutual fund went up in price or how much the shares have yielded, extra effort must be taken to make sure that the ad is not misleading. To accomplish this, it's usually sensible or necessary to include a statement to the effect that past performance cannot be taken as indication of future performance and that some risk is involved.

UNIT INVESTMENT TRUSTS

Similar information may be included in ads for other investment vehicles registered under the Investment Company Act of 1940, such as unit investment trusts, another widely advertised class of investment company. A unit investment trust differs from a mutual fund principally in that the securities in the fund are not managed. Today the holdings of practically all unit investment trusts consist of bonds, mostly municipal bonds. When the trust is formed, shares are sold to the public. When the trust is dissolved, the principal is returned to investors. (See the Nuveen advertisements in Chapter 6.)

An advertisement for a unit investment trust may contain all the information that a mutual fund ad may, with appropriate modification.

BROKERAGE FIRMS

All the above restrictions on investment company advertising apply if the name of one or more of the mutual funds or unit investment trusts appears in the advertisement. But when mutual funds in general or other classes of investment companies in general are advertised, as brokerage firms do from time to time, the restrictions are much, much fewer. In fact, in creating or judging a so-called generic investment company ad, one must principally be careful that the ad does not slip into advertising a specific investment company or companies.

If the advertiser intends to send respondents a booklet and/or other information that aims to cause them to buy shares in one or more specific mutual funds, not only must a prospectus or prospectuses be sent along with the fulfilling material, but also additional language must be included in the ad, stating (1) the number of investment companies about which information can be obtained (but not the names of the investment companies—that would make the ad subject to Rule 134) and (2) that the advertiser underwrites, distributes, or advises any of the investment companies (if the advertiser does sponsor and/or manage and/or advise). Acceptable language fulfilling both (1) and (2) would be: ''For complete information about either or both of the funds we advise and distribute, telephone or mail the coupon.''

The rules for generic mutual fund advertisements are so liberal that the writer or judge can't go far wrong if he or she follows the guidelines above and keeps within the rules of the New York Stock Exchange.

MEMBERS OF THE NEW YORK STOCK EXCHANGE

Even if an advertiser is not a member of the New York Stock Exchange, adhering to NYSE rules can be beneficial, because doing so may minimize the possibility that the advertiser will be sued for fraud or be censured by one of the regulatory bodies.

The most important prohibition in NYSE rules states that no advertisement or other communication by a member firm shall contain "promises of specific results" or "exaggerated or unwarranted claims."

Another important provision states that no ad may contain "opinions for which there is no reasonable basis."

The NYSE also requires that all forecasts and projections must be labeled as such—again to make sure that investors are not misled into believing that they are sure to obtain those results.

At one time, no NYSE member firm could compare its service with that of another member. Currently, however, the rules allow such comparisons, but insist that comparisons be "factually supportable."

A firm that wants to brag about how well its stock recommendations have turned out can do so, as long as the record is portrayed in a fair and balanced manner. Regulations similar to those that affect mutual fund ads which include performance figures apply—particularly that figures or graphs need to be for at least the most recent 12-month period.

The New York Stock Exchange does allow testimonials, but restrictions reduce their effectiveness. On top of the FTC requirements, described in the bank regulation chapter, a testimonial concerning the quality of a firm's investment advice must state (1) that whatever the endorser says may not be representative of the experience of other clients and (2) that what has been done for the endorser may not be indicative of future performance or success. In addition, if the endorser is paid more than a nominal amount, the fact that it is a paid testimonial must be indicated.

E. F. Hutton placed one of the few brokerage testimonial ads on television in the early 1970s. It featured J. Paul Getty.

IN PRACTICE

As you can see, for a novice to absorb all this information and then create a legally acceptable advertisement, or to judge whether an ad is legally acceptable, would be difficult. In real life, the organization which the writer or executive joins usually has some experience in what is legally acceptable and what is not. Effective advertisements that have been approved by compliance people may be available for inspection—as well as, perhaps, some that were disallowed.

Often the writer must use weaker constructions that he or she has learned to eschew when learning how to write forcefully. "May" and "could" might have to be substituted for "can"; "would" substituted for "will"; "should" substituted for "shall." Sometimes "can," "will," and "shall" can be used if the statement is qualified in some other way, such as adding "we believe," "in our judgment," "usually," "sometimes" or "often". Colorful adjectives are seldom acceptable. Qualifying adjectives can sometimes make a strong noun acceptable; "growth" cannot be promised, but "a stock with *potential* growth" can be recommended.

Often ingenuity in an investment advertisement is not apparent except to those who have tried to write, or get from their agency, ads that are both highly effective and legally acceptable.

14

INSURANCE ADVERTISING REGULATIONS

To obtain some uniformity in regulation of insurance advertising among the several states, the National Association of Insurance Commissioners (NAIC) has developed model rules, which have been adopted in whole or in part by many states. This chapter will concern itself with the NAIC's model rules.

Even if a company does not do business in a state that has these rules, following them will not only insure that the advertising is ethical but also help prevent the company from being sued because of misrepresentation.

Even more than for bank and investment advertising, the rules governing insurance advertising stress that the advertising must be truthful and not misleading in fact or by implication. If something is left out that could result in a person of average education or intelligence being misled, the ad is illegal. The fact that a policy is made available for inspection before the insurance is bought, or that there is an offer to refund the premium if the insurer is not satisfied, does not remedy misleading statements. Words and phrases that would be clear and meaningful only to people familiar with insurance terminology are not to be used.

The rules outlaw a host of words and phrases that are tempting to use but that may mislead. Most of them apply to the advertising of specific health policies, but the point they make applies to all insurance advertising. Here are some examples:

"The finest kind of treatment" can't be used, because it may imply that such treatment would not be obtained without insurance.

"Low," "low cost," "budget," "only," "just," etc., cannot be used to describe the cost of insurance when the premiums are low because of limited coverage or few benefits.

"New," "breakthrough," etc., cannot be used when the type of policy has been in existence for some time,

"All," "full," "complete," etc., can seldom be used, particularly in reference to benefits.

"Extra," "special," and "added" cannot be used to describe any benefit.

"Only," "just," "merely," and similar minimizers cannot be used to describe any exceptions or modifications.

"Liberal," "generous," etc., cannot be used to describe claim settlements.

"Financial disaster" or a similar phrase cannot be used to describe what a policy might prevent when the policy offers only limited coverage.

The copywriter must be especially careful to make sure that all the limitations involved are stated. For example, if coverage for a sickness includes staying in a hospital but not in a nursing home, that fact must be stated. If benefits vary by age, that fact must be stated.

Captions such as "Lifetime Sickness Benefits" are incomplete if such benefits are subject to confinement requirements. "Lifetime House Confining Sickness Benefits" would be permissible.

Similarly, stressing the importance of diseases not common in the class of persons to whom the policy is offered should not be exaggerated.

"Cancer kills somebody every two minutes" violates the NAIC model rules, but inclusion of accurate statistics does not. "Here is where most people over 65 learn about gaps in Medicare" is not permissible, but a dispassionate, accurate statement of supplemental benefits is.

Copywriters of insurance advertising need to carefully apply their abilities to stimulate emotion. If the horrors of an accident or sickness are exaggerated, the ad may be not only in violation of regulations, but also less effective than otherwise. Instead of driving readers to send for more information or to mail in a premium, such a strong negative emotion may be aroused that the reader, viewer, or listener wants to think of something else.

Writers of direct mail and coupon advertisements must avoid two temptations. One is to say something like "Because no commission is paid to an agent, this is a low-cost plan" or "We save you money because we deal directly with you." The policy or the company must be sold on its other merits.

The other temptation springs from the current desire on the part of the copywriter to give readers, viewers, or listeners a reason for acting immediately. An NAIC rule specifically states: "An advertisement shall not state or imply that only a specific number of policies will be sold, or that a time is fixed for the discontinuance of the sale of the particular policy advertised because of special advantages available in the policy."

The rules frown on comparative advertising, but these particular rules might not be upheld by the U.S. Supreme Court. Obviously, the advertising should not make unfair or incomplete comparisons of policies, benefits, dividends, or rates of other insurers. Fulfilling this criterion may prove difficult because of the many conditions involved in any insurance policy. So, at least, copywriters and judges of insurance advertising need to be wary of comparative advertising.

Any implication that a prospect may realize a profit by buying the insurance should be avoided. The profit motive cannot be aroused even indirectly, such as implying that buyers of the insurance will get free trips to Florida if they get sick.

The rules cannot be circumvented by the use of illustrations instead of words. To prevent readers from feeling they will make a profit, the rules forbid depicting currency or checks showing an amount payable. And coupons cannot be made to look like currency.

In addition, illustrations should not unduly emphasize automobile accidents, cripples or persons confined to beds in obvious distress, and the like.

Testimonials are permitted, but some rigid restraints apply when an advertisement features a specific insurance policy. Testimonials about how good the insurance company is in general, how it pays claims promptly, etc., need only subscribe to the Federal Trade Commission regulations, which are summarized in Chapter 12.

If a specific policy is endorsed, however, the following rules apply (which usually make it better to use some other kind of advertising):

If the person making the testimonial or an appraisal has a financial interest in the insurer or a related entity as a stockholder, director, officer, employee, or otherwise, such fact shall be disclosed in the advertisement. If the endorser is paid more than union wages, that fact must be disclosed. Two words suffice—"Paid Endorsement." Even if the payment is only free travel and/or entertainment, the two words must be included. The words should be in type style and size identical to the endorser's name.

The best way to judge an insurance advertisement is to consider the ad an insurance policy—that is, to suppose that a prospect buys the insurance based solely on the advertising and when, say, he or she suffers a loss and is told that it is not covered, he or she sues and appears before a consumer-minded judge and jury. This has happened, and courts have held that the promises in the advertisement must be kept by the insurance company.

Part III

88 AGENCIES WITH FINANCIAL SERVICES ADVERTISING EXPERIENCE

15

AGENCIES WITH FINANCIAL ADVERTISING EXPERIENCE HEADQUARTERED OR WITH AN OFFICE IN NEW YORK CITY

Entries are listed alphabetically by agency

AC&R Advertising Inc.
Experienced in: direct response and visit-our-office advertising
Founded: 1965
16 East Thirty-second Street
New York, NY 10016

Albert Frank–Guenther Law Incorporated
Experienced in: bank, investment, insurance, image, direct response, visit-our-office, and tombstone advertising
Founded: 1872
61 Broadway
New York, NY 10006
Other offices in Philadelphia and San Francisco

Ally & Gargano
Experienced in: bank, insurance, image, direct response, visit-our-office, and tombstone advertising
Founded: 1962
805 Third Avenue
New York, NY 10022

N W Ayer Incorporated
Experienced in: bank, investment, insurance, image, direct response, visit-our-office, and tombstone advertising
Founded: 1869
1345 Avenue of the Americas
New York, NY 10105
Other offices in Chicago, Detroit, and Los Angeles

Ted Bates Advertising/New York
Experienced in: insurance image advertising
1515 Broadway
New York, NY 10036

Batten, Barton, Durstine & Osborn, Inc.
Experienced in: bank, investment, image, and visit-our-office advertising
Founded: 1891
383 Madison Avenue
New York, NY 10017
Other offices in Atlanta, Beaverton (OR), Los Angeles, Minneapolis, San Francisco, and Southfield (MI)

BBDO Direct
Experienced in: bank direct response advertising
Founded: 1982
385 Madison Avenue
New York, NY 10017

Benn & MacDonough, Inc.
Experienced in: bank, investment, insurance, image, direct response, visit-our-office, and tombstone advertising
Case histories following Chapter 1 (a discount broker), following Chapter 2 (Municipal Bond Insurance Association and Diamond Portfolio Ltd.), following Chapter 6 (John Nuveen & Co. Incorporated), following Chapter 7 (Bank of Boston International), and in Chapter 9 (PaineWebber Incorporated and a corporate bond fund)
Founded: 1967
111 Broadway
New York, NY 10006

Bozell, Jacobs, Kenyon & Eckhardt, Inc.
Experienced in: bank, investment, insurance, image, direct response, and tombstone advertising
Case history in Chapter 10 (Citizens & Southern Bank of South Carolina)
One Dag Hammarskjold Plaza
New York, NY 10017
Other offices in Alexandria (VA), Atlanta, Beaverton (OR), Birmingham (MI), Boston, Braintree (MA), Chicago, Cincinnati, Dallas, Denver, Houston, Kansas City (MO), Los Angeles, Memphis, Metairie (LA), Minneapolis, Oak Brook (IL), Omaha, Orlando, Phoenix, Pittsburgh, St. Ann (MO), Salt Lake City, San Ramon (CA), Syracuse, and Union (NJ)

Brouillard Communications (Division of J. Walter Thompson)
Experienced in: bank, investment, insurance, image, and direct response advertising
Case history in Chapter 5 (Irving Trust)
Founded: 1975

420 Lexington Avenue
New York, NY 10017
Other office in Pittsburgh

Cunningham & Walsh, Inc.
Experienced in: bank, insurance, image, and direct response advertising
Founded: 1950
260 Madison Avenue
New York, NY 10016
Other offices in Chicago and Fountain Valley (CA)

Dancer Fitzgerald Sample, Inc.
Experienced in: bank, insurance, image, and visit-our-office advertising
Founded: 1924
405 Lexington Avenue
New York, NY 10174
Other offices in San Francisco and Torrance (CA)

D'Arcy Masius Benton & Bowles Inc.
Experienced in: bank, investment, insurance, image, and direct response
    advertising
Case history following Chapter 7 (E. F. Hutton & Company)
Founded: 1929
909 Third Avenue
New York, NY 10022
Other offices in Atlanta, Bloomfield Hills (MI), Bloomington (MN), Chicago,
    Houston, Los Angeles, St. Louis, and San Francisco.

Della Femina, Travisano & Partners, Inc.
Experienced in: bank, investment, image, and visit-our-office advertising
Founded: 1967
625 Madison Avenue
New York, NY 10022
Other office in Los Angeles

The Direct Marketing Group, Inc.
Experienced in: bank, investment, insurance, and direct response advertising
Founded: 1973
477 Madison Avenue
New York, NY 10022

Doremus & Company
Experienced in: bank, investment, insurance, image, direct response, and tomb-
    stone advertising
Case history following Chapter 2 (Standard & Poor's)
Founded: 1903
120 Broadway
New York, NY 10271
Other offices in Boston, Chicago, Los Angeles, San Francisco, and Washington, D.C.

Doyle Dane Bernbach Group Inc.
Experienced in: bank, investment, insurance, image, and visit-our-office advertising
Case history in Chapter 1 (CIGNA)
Founded: 1949
437 Madison Avenue
New York, NY 10022
Other offices in Denver, Los Angeles, Rosemont (IL), San Francisco, and Troy (MI)

Doyle Graf Mabley
Experienced in: bank, investment, insurance, image, direct response, and visit-our-office advertising
Case history in Chapter 4 (The Morgan Bank)
Founded: 1959
600 Third Avenue
New York, NY 10016

DYR Inc.
Experienced in: bank and direct response advertising
Founded: 1983
1114 Avenue of the Americas
New York, NY 10036
Other office in Los Angeles

William Esty Company Incorporated
Experienced in: bank, insurance, image, and direct response advertising
Founded: 1932
100 East Forty-second Street
New York, NY 10017
Other office in Los Angeles

Fairfax Advertising, Inc.
Experienced in: investment, insurance, image, and direct response advertising
635 Madison Avenue
New York, NY 10022

Foote, Cone & Belding Communications, Inc.
Experienced in: bank, insurance, image, and visit-our-office advertising
Founded: 1873
101 Park Avenue
New York, NY 10178
Other offices in Chicago, Los Angeles, and San Francisco

Geer, DuBois Advertising, Inc.
Experienced in: bank, investment, and insurance image advertising
Founded: 1946
114 Fifth Avenue
New York, NY 10011

Grey Advertising Inc.
Experienced in: bank, investment, insurance, image, direct response, and visit-our-office advertising
Case history in and following Chapter 1 (Bank of America)
Founded: 1917
777 Third Avenue
New York, NY 10017
Other offices in Chicago, Minneapolis, Los Angeles, and San Francisco

HBM/Creamer
Experienced in: bank, insurance, image, and visit-our-office advertising
Founded: 1916
Paramount Plaza
1633 Broadway
New York, NY 10019
Other offices in Boston, Chicago, Pittsburgh, Hartford, Providence (RI), and Washington, D.C.

Hicks & Greist, Inc.
Experienced in: bank, investment, insurance, image, direct response, visit-our-office, and tombstone advertising
Founded: 1956
220 East Forty-second Street
New York, NY 10017

Ketchum Communications, Inc.
Experienced in: bank, investment, insurance, image, and direct response advertising
Case histories in Chapter 9 (Pittsburgh National Bank and Union Trust Bank)
1133 Avenue of the Americas
New York, NY 10036
Other offices in Chicago, Houston, Los Angeles, Philadelphia, Pittsburgh, Rockville (MD), and San Francisco

Kornhauser & Calene, Inc.
Experienced in: bank, investment, insurance, image, direct response, visit-our-office, and tombstone advertising
Founded: 1980
228 East Forty-fifth Street
New York, NY 10017

Laurence, Charles, Free, & Lawson
Experienced in: investment direct response advertising
Founded: 1952
261 Madison Avenue
New York, NY 10016

Leber Katz Partners
Experienced in: investment, insurance, image, and direct response advertising
Founded: 1954
767 Fifth Avenue
New York, NY 10153

Al Paul Lefton Co., Inc.
Experienced in: insurance direct response and visit-our-office advertising
Founded: 1928
71 Vanderbilt Avenue
New York, NY 10169
Other office in Philadelphia

Levine, Huntley, Schmidt & Beaver, Inc.
Experienced in: bank image advertising
Founded: 1972
250 Park Avenue, 11th Floor
New York, NY 10177

Lord, Geller, Federico, Einstein, Inc.
Experienced in: bank, investment, insurance, image, direct response, and visit-our-office advertising
Founded: 1967
655 Madison Avenue
New York, NY 10021
Other office in Boca Raton (FL)

McCaffrey and McCall, Inc.
Experienced in: bank, investment, insurance, image, direct response, and visit-our-office advertising
Founded: 1962
575 Lexington Avenue
New York, NY 10022

McCann Erickson Inc.
Experienced in: bank, investment, insurance, image, and visit-our-office advertising
485 Lexington Avenue
New York, NY 10017
Other offices in Atlanta, Dallas, Houston, Louisville (KY), Los Angeles, San Francisco, Seattle, and Troy (MI)

Mandabach & Simms, Inc.
Experienced in: bank, investment, image, and direct response advertising
801 Second Avenue
New York, NY 10017
Other offices in Chicago, Emeryville (CA), Fort Lauderdale, and Mansfield (OH)

Marschalk Company (The)

Experienced in: bank, investment, insurance, image, and visit-our-office advertising
Founded: 1924
1345 Avenue of the Americas
New York, NY 10105
Other offices in Cleveland, Houston, and San Francisco

Mast Advertising Associates, Inc.

Experienced in: bank and investment direct response advertising
Case history following Chapter 7 (Citibank)
Founded: 1975
6 East Forty-fifth Street
New York, NY 10017

Needham Harper Worldwide, Inc.

Experienced in: bank, investment, insurance, image, visit-our-office, and direct response advertising
Founded: 1925
909 Third Avenue
New York, NY 10022
Other offices in Chicago, Los Angeles, San Diego, Phoenix, and McLean (VA)

Ogilvy & Mather Advertising

Experienced in: bank, investment, insurance, image, direct response, and tombstone advertising
Case histories following Chapter 3 (California First Bank) and Chapter 5 (Nationwide Insurance)
Founded: 1977
675 Third Avenue
New York, NY 10017
Other offices in Atlanta, Chicago, Dallas, Houston, Los Angeles, San Francisco, and Washington, D.C.

Rosenfeld, Sirowitz & Humphrey, Inc.

Experienced in: bank, investment, insurance, image, and direct response advertising
Founded: 1971
111 Fifth Avenue
New York, NY 10003

Rumrill-Hoyt, Inc.

Experienced in: bank, image, direct response, and tombstone advertising
Founded: 1933
635 Madison Avenue
New York, NY 10022
Other office in Rochester (NY)

Saatchi & Saatchi Compton Inc.
Experienced in: investment, insurance, image, and direct response advertising
Founded: 1908
625 Madison Avenue
New York, NY 10022
Other office in Southfield (MI)

Soskin/Thompson Associates
Experienced in: bank, investment, and insurance direct response advertising
420 Lexington Avenue
New York, NY 10017
Other offices in Chicago, Los Angeles, and San Francisco

SSC&B:Lintas USA
Experienced in: bank, investment, image, and direct response advertising
Founded: 1946
One Dag Hammarskjold Plaza
New York, NY 10017

SZF, Inc.
Experienced in: bank, investment, image, and direct response advertising
Founded: 1968
104 Fifth Avenue
New York, NY 10011

J. Walter Thompson U.S.A., Inc.
Experienced in: bank, investment, insurance, image, and visit-our-office
  advertising
Founded: 1864
466 Lexington Avenue
New York, NY 10017
Other offices in Atlanta, Bala Cynwyd (PA), Charlotte (NC), Chicago, Coconut
  Grove (FL), Dallas, Denver, Detroit, Fairport (NY), Houston, Indianapolis,
  Los Angeles, Louisville, Memphis, New Orleans, Oklahoma City, Omaha,
  Overland Park (KS), Phoenix, Richmond (VA), St. Ann (MO), Salt Lake
  City, San Francisco, and Washington, D.C.

Vitale Advertising Group Inc.
Experienced in: bank image and visit-our-office advertising
Ad in Chapter 12
Founded: 1961
114 East Thirty-second Street
New York, NY 10016

Waring & LaRosa, Inc.
Experienced in: investment and insurance image advertising
Founded: 1968
555 Madison Avenue
New York, NY 10022

Wells, Rich, Greene, Inc.
Experienced in: bank image and visit-our-office advertising
Founded: 1966
767 Fifth Avenue
New York, NY 10153
Other offices in Los Angeles, Detroit, and Chicago

Winkler/McDermott/Winkler, Inc.
Experienced in: bank, investment, insurance, image, and direct response
  advertising
Founded: 1983
65 Bleecker Street
New York, NY 10012

Wunderman, Ricotta & Kline Incorporated
Experienced in: bank and investment direct response advertising
Founded: 1958
575 Madison Avenue
New York, NY 10022
Other office in Detroit

Wyse Advertising, Inc.
Experienced in: bank and image advertising
505 Park Avenue
New York, NY 10022
Other offices in Cleveland and Los Angeles

Young & Rubicam, Inc.
Experienced in: bank, investment, image, and visit-our-office advertising
Founded: 1923
285 Madison Avenue
New York, NY 10017
Other offices in Chicago, Detroit, and San Francisco

16

AGENCIES WITH FINANCIAL ADVERTISING EXPERIENCE HEADQUARTERED OR WITH OFFICES *OUTSIDE* NEW YORK CITY

Entries are listed alphabetically by state, city, and agency

ARIZONA

Phoenix

Bozell, Jacobs, Kenyon & Eckhardt, Inc.
Experienced in: bank, investment, insurance, image, direct response, and tombstone advertising
Case history in Chapter 10 (Citizens & Southern Bank of South Carolina)
Founded: 1921
100 West Clarendon Avenue, Suite 2206
Phoenix, AZ 85013

Evans/Motta, Inc.
Experienced in: bank, investment, insurance, image, direct response, visit-our-office, and tombstone advertising
2122 East Highland Avenue, Suite 400
Phoenix, AZ 85016

Needham Harper Worldwide, USA, Inc.
Experienced in: bank, insurance, image, and visit-our-office advertising
2141 East Highland Avenue, Suite 200
Phoenix, AZ 85016

J. Walter Thompson U.S.A., Inc.
Experienced in: bank, investment, insurance, image, and visit-our-office advertising

3003 North Central Avenue, Suite 1200
Phoenix, AZ 85012

ARKANSAS

Little Rock

Combs & Company
Experienced in: bank and insurance advertising
201 West Third Street, Suite 300
Little Rock, AR 72201

CALIFORNIA

Emeryville

Mandabach & Simms, Inc.
Experienced in: bank, investment, image, direct response, and visit-our-office
advertising
1201 Park Avenue
Emeryville, CA 94068

Fountain Valley

Cunningham & Walsh Inc.
Experienced in: bank, insurance, image, and direct response advertising
10540 Talbert Avenue, Suite 250
Fountain Valley, CA 92708

Los Angeles

N W Ayer Incorporated
Experienced in: bank, investment, insurance, image, direct response, visit-our-
office, and tombstone advertising
707 Wilshire Boulevard
Los Angeles, CA 90017

BBDO/West
Experienced in: bank, investment, image, and visit-our-office advertising
10960 Wilshire Boulevard
Los Angeles, CA 90024

Bozell, Jacobs, Kenyon & Eckhardt, Inc.

Experienced in: bank, investment, insurance, image, direct response, and tombstone advertising
Case history in Chapter 10 (Citizens & Southern Bank of South Carolina)
10850 Wilshire Boulevard
Los Angeles, CA 90024

Bozell, Jacobs, Kenyon & Eckhárdt, Inc.

Experienced in: bank, investment, insurance, direct response, and tombstone advertising
Case history in Chapter 10 (Citizens & Southern Bank of South Carolina)
1100 Glendon Avenue, Suite 715
Los Angeles, CA 90024

Chiat/Day Inc.

Experienced in: bank and investment image advertising
Founded: 1968
517 South Olive Street
Los Angeles, CA 90013

D'Arcy Masius Benton & Bowles Inc.

Experienced in: bank, investment, insurance, image, and direct response advertising
Case history following Chapter 7 (E. F. Hutton & Company)
3435 Wilshire Boulevard
Los Angeles, CA 90010

Davis, Johnson, Mogul & Colombatto, Inc.

Experienced in: bank, investment, insurance, image, direct response, visit-our-office, and tombstone advertising
Founded: 1957
3435 Wilshire Boulevard, 18th Floor
Los Angeles, CA 90010

Della Femina, Travisano & Partners of California Inc.

Experienced in: bank, investment, image, and visit-our-office advertising
5900 Wilshire Boulevard
Los Angeles, CA 90036

W. B. Doner & Company

Experienced in: bank, image, and direct response advertising
10850 Wilshire Boulevard, Suite 210
Los Angeles, CA 90024

Doremus & Company

Experienced in: bank, investment, insurance, image, direct response, and tombstone advertising
Case history following Chapter 2 (Standard & Poor's)
10960 Wilshire Boulevard, Suite 1422
Los Angeles, CA 90024

Doyle Dane Bernbach Group Inc.

Experienced in: bank, investment, insurance, image, and visit-our-office advertising
Case history in Chapter 1 (CIGNA)
5900 Wilshire Boulevard
Los Angeles, CA 90036

DYR Inc.

Experienced in: bank direct response advertising
4751 Wilshire Boulevard
Los Angeles, CA 90010

William Esty Company, Inc.

Experienced in: bank, insurance, image, and direct response advertising
9841 Airport Boulevard
Los Angeles, CA 90045

Evans/Weinberg, Inc.

Experienced in: bank, investment, insurance, image, direct response, visit-our-office, and tombstone advertising
Museum Square Penthouse
5757 Wilshire Boulevard
Los Angeles, CA 90036

Foote, Cone & Belding Communications, Inc.

Experienced in: bank, insurance, image, and visit-our-office advertising
11601 Wilshire Boulevard
Los Angeles, CA 90025

Grey Advertising Inc.

Experienced in: bank, investment, insurance, image, direct response, and visit-our-office advertising
Case history in and after Chapter 1 (Bank of America)
3435 Wilshire Boulevard
Los Angeles, CA 90010

Gumpertz/Bentley/Fried

Experienced in: bank and investment advertising
Case history following Chapter 7 (National Enterprise Bank)
Founded: 1959
5900 Wilshire Boulevard
Los Angeles, CA 90036

Hill, Holliday, Connors, Cosmopulos, Inc.

Experienced in: bank, investment, insurance, image, and direct response advertising
2029 Century Park East, Suite 830
Los Angeles, CA 90067

Ketchum Communications, Inc.
Experienced in: bank, investment, insurance, image, and direct response
  advertising
Case histories in Chapter 9 (Pittsburgh National Bank and Union Trust Bank)
3250 Wilshire Boulevard, Suite 1402
Los Angeles, CA 90010

McCann Erickson Inc.
Experienced in: bank, investment, insurance, image, and visit-our-office
  advertising
6420 Wilshire Boulevard
Los Angeles, CA 90048

Needham Harper Worldwide, Inc.
Experienced in: bank, insurance, image, and visit-our-office advertising
Kirkeby Center, 11601 Wilshire Boulevard
Los Angeles, CA 90025

Ogilvy & Mather Advertising
Experienced in: bank, investment, insurance, image, direct response, and tomb-
  stone advertising
Case histories following Chapter 3 (California First Bank) and Chapter 5
  (Nationwide Insurance)
5757 Wilshire Boulevard
Los Angeles, CA 90036

Soskin/Thompson Associates
Experienced in: bank, investment, and insurance direct response advertising
10100 Santa Monica Boulevard
Los Angeles, CA 90067

J. Walter Thompson U.S.A., Inc.
Experienced in: bank, investment, insurance, image, and visit-our-office
  advertising
10100 Santa Monica Boulevard
Los Angeles, CA 90067

Wells, Rich, Greene/West
Experienced in: bank, image, and visit-our-office advertising
2029 Century Park East
Los Angeles, CA 90067

Wunderman West (Division of DYR Inc.)
Experienced in: bank and investment direct response advertising
4751 Wilshire Boulevard
Los Angeles, CA 90010

Wyse Advertising, Inc.
Experienced in: bank and image advertising
9841 Airport Boulevard, Suite 410
Los Angeles, CA 90045

Newport Beach

Cochrane Chase Livingston & Co.
Experienced in: investment, insurance, image, and direct response advertising
5 Civic Plaza, P.O. Box 8710
Newport Beach, CA 92658

San Diego

Davis, Johnson, Mogul & Colombatto, Inc.
Experienced in: bank, investment, insurance, image, direct response, visit-our-office, and tombstone advertising
4501 Mission Bay Drive
San Diego, CA 92109

Needham Harper Worldwide, Inc.
Experienced in: bank, insurance, image, and visit-our-office advertising
876 Arrow Drive South, Suite 225
San Diego, CA 92123

San Francisco

Batten, Barton, Durstine & Osborn, Inc.
Experienced in: bank, investment, image, and visit-our-office advertising
825 Battery Street
San Francisco, CA 94111

Chiat/Day Inc.
Experienced in: bank and investment image advertising
414 Jackson Square
San Francisco, CA 94111

Dancer Fitzgerald Sample, Inc.
Experienced in: bank, insurance, image, and visit-our-office advertising
1010 Battery Street
San Francisco, CA 94111

D'Arcy Masius Benton & Bowles Inc.
Experienced in: bank, insurance, image, and direct response advertising
433 California Street
San Francisco, CA 94104

Davis, Johnson, Mogul & Colombatto, Inc.
Experienced in: bank, investment, insurance, image, direct response, visit-our-office, and tombstone advertising
27 Maiden Lane
San Francisco, CA 94108

Doremus & Company
Experienced in: bank, investment, insurance, image, direct response, and tombstone advertising
Case history following Chapter 2 (Standard & Poor's)
825 Battery Street
San Francisco, CA 94111

Doyle Dane Bernbach Group Inc.
Experienced in: bank, investment, insurance, image, and visit-our-office advertising
Case history in Chapter 1 (CIGNA)
530 Bush Street
San Francisco, CA 94108

Evans/Lynch Rockey, Inc.
Experienced in: bank, investment, insurance, image, direct response, visit-our-office, and tombstone advertising
535 Pacific Avenue
San Francisco, CA 94133

Foote, Cone & Belding Communications, Inc.
Experienced in: bank, investment, insurance, image, direct response, and visit-our-office advertising
1255 Battery Street
San Francisco, CA 94111

Grey Advertising Inc.
Experienced in: bank, investment, insurance, image, direct response, and visit-our-office advertising
Case history in and after Chapter 1 (Bank of America)
50 California Street
San Francisco, CA 94111

Ketchum Communications, Inc.
Experienced in: bank, investment, insurance, image, and direct response advertising
Case histories in Chapter 9 (Pittsburgh National Bank and Union Trust Bank)
55 Union Street
San Francisco, CA 94111

McCann Erickson Inc.
Experienced in: bank, investment, insurance, image, and visit-our-office advertising
201 California Street
San Francisco, CA 94111

Marschalk Company (The)
Experienced in: bank, investment, insurance, and image advertising
574 Pacific Avenue
San Francisco, CA 94133

Ogilvy & Mather Advertising
Experienced in: bank, investment, insurance, image, direct response, and tombstone advertising.
735 Battery Street
San Francisco, CA 94111

Soskin/Thompson Associates West Coast
Experienced in: bank, investment, and insurance direct response advertising
Four Embarcadero Center, Suite 700
San Francisco, CA 94111

J. Walter Thompson U.S.A. Inc.
Experienced in: bank, investment, insurance, image, and visit-our-office advertising
Four Embarcadero Center, Suite 900
San Francisco, CA 94111

Young & Rubicam San Francisco
Experienced in: bank, investment, image, and visit-our-office advertising
753 Davis Street
San Francisco, CA 94111

San Ramon

Bozell, Jacobs, Kenyon & Eckhardt, Inc.
Experienced in: bank, investment, insurance, image, and visit-our-office advertising
Case history in Chapter 10 (Citizens & Southern Bank of South Carolina)
7 Crow Canyon Court, Suite 209
San Ramon, CA 94583

Torrance

Dancer Fitzgerald Sample, Inc.
Experienced in: bank, insurance, image, and visit-our-office advertising
Del Amo Executive Plaza
3878 Carson Street
Torrance, CA 90503

COLORADO

Denver

Bozell, Jacobs, Kenyon & Eckhardt, Inc.
Experienced in: bank, investment, insurance, image, and visit-our-office advertising

Case history in Chapter 10 (Citizens & Southern Bank of South Carolina)
1380 Lawrence Street, Suite 890
Denver, CO 80204

Doyle Dane Bernbach Group Inc.
Experienced in: bank, investment, insurance, image, and visit-our-office
  advertising
Case history in Chapter 1 (CIGNA)
2 Tamarac Square Building
7535 East Hampden Avenue, Suite 416
Denver, CO 80231

Evans/Bartholomew, Inc.
Experienced in: bank, investment, insurance, image, direct response, visit-our-
  office, and tombstone advertising
2128 Fifteenth Street
Denver, CO 80202

J. Walter Thompson U.S.A., Inc.
Experienced in: bank, investment, insurance, image, and visit-our-office
  advertising
300 South Jackson Street
Denver, CO 80209

Englewood

Colle & McVoy Advertising Group, Inc.
Experienced in: bank, investment, insurance, image, visit-our-office, and direct
  response advertising
6900 East Bellview Avenue
Englewood, CO 80111

Tracy-Locke Advertising, Inc.
Experienced in: bank, investment, insurance, image, direct response, visit-our-
  office, and tombstone advertising
7503 Marin Drive
Plaza Marin III, Suite B
Englewood, CO 80111

CONNECTICUT

Avon

Mintz & Hoke Inc.
Experienced in: bank, investment, insurance, image, direct response, visit-our-
  office, and tombstone advertising

Case history in Chapter 3 (Connecticut Bank & Trust Company)
Founded: 1971
40 Tower Lane
Avon, CT 06001

Hartford

HBM/Creamer, Inc.
Experienced in: bank, insurance, image, and visit-our-office advertising
100 Constitution Plaza
Hartford, CT 06103

Stratford

Merrill Anderson Co. Inc.
Experienced in: bank and direct response advertising
Founded: 1934
1166 Barnum Avenue
Stratford, CT 06497

DISTRICT OF COLUMBIA

Doremus & Company
Experienced in: bank, investment, insurance, image, direct response, and tombstone advertising
Case history following Chapter 2 (Standard & Poor's)
655 Fifteenth Street NW
Washington, DC 20005

HBM/Creamer, Inc.
Experienced in: bank, insurance, image, and visit-our-office advertising
1612 K Street NW, Suite 706
Washington, DC 20006

Ogilvy & Mather Advertising
Experienced in: bank, investment, insurance, image, direct response, and tombstone advertising
Case histories following Chapter 3 (California First Bank) and Chapter 5 (Nationwide Insurance)
1901 L Street NW, Suite 320
Washington, DC 20036

J. Walter Thompson U.S.A., Inc.
Experienced in: bank, investment, insurance, image, and visit-our-office advertising
1156 Fifteenth Street NW
Washington, DC 20005

FLORIDA

Boca Raton

Lord, Geller, Federico, Einstein Inc.
Experienced in: bank, investment, insurance, image, direct response, and visit-our-office advertising
1515 North Federal Highway
Boca Raton, FL 33432

Coconut Grove

J. Walter Thompson U.S.A., Inc.
Experienced in: bank, investment, insurance, image, and visit-our-office advertising
3250 Mary Street, Suite 203
Coconut Grove, FL 33133

Coral Gables

Colle & McVoy Advertising Agency, Inc.
Experienced in: bank, investment, insurance, image, visit-our-office, and direct response advertising
301 Almeria Avenue
Coral Gables, FL 33134

Fort Lauderdale

Manchester Marketing, Inc. (Affiliate of Mandabach & Simms, Inc.)
Experienced in: bank, investment, image, direct response, and visit-our-office advertising
5300 Powerline Road, Suite 212
Fort Lauderdale, FL 33309

Orlando

Bozell, Jacobs, Kenyon & Eckhardt, Inc.
Experienced in: bank, investment, insurance, image, and visit-our-office advertising
Case history in Chapter 10 (Citizens & Southern Bank of South Carolina)
7000 Lake Ellenor Drive, Suite 115
Orlando, FL 32809

Pompano Beach

Group 3hree Advertising Corporation
Experienced in: bank, investment, image, direct response, visit-our-office, and tombstone advertising
Founded: 1971
3200 Northeast Fourteenth Street Causeway
Pompano Beach, FL 33062

St. Petersburg

W. B. Doner & Company
Experienced in: bank, image, and direct response advertising
9455 Koger Boulevard, Suite 200
St. Petersburg, FL 33702

GEORGIA

Atlanta

Batten, Barton, Durstine & Osborn, Inc.
Experienced in: bank, investment, image, and visit-our-office advertising
3414 Peachtree Road NE
Atlanta, GA 30326

Bozell, Jacobs, Kenyon & Eckhardt, Inc.
Experienced in: bank, investment, insurance, image, direct response, visit-our-office, and tombstone advertising
Case history in Chapter 10 (Citizens & Southern Bank of South Carolina)
400 Colony Square, No. 1833
Atlanta, GA 30361

D'Arcy Masius Benton & Bowles Inc.
Experienced in: bank, insurance, image, and direct response advertising
400 Colony Square NE, Suite 1901
Atlanta, GA 30361

Evans Communications/Atlanta
Experienced in: bank, investment, insurance, image, direct response, visit-our-office, and tombstone advertising
Pharr Center, 500 Pharr Road
Atlanta, GA 30363

Fletcher/Mayo/Associates Inc.
Experienced in: bank, investment, insurance, image, direct response, and visit-our-office advertising

5 Piedmont Center, Suite 710
Atlanta, GA 30305

McCann Erickson Inc.
Experienced in: bank, investment, insurance, image, and visit-our-office
   advertising
615 Peachtree Street, NE
Atlanta, GA 30365

Ogilvy & Mather Advertising
Experienced in: bank, investment, insurance, image, direct response, and tomb-
   stone advertising
Case histories following Chapter 3 (California First Bank) and Chapter 5 (Na-
   tionwide Insurance)
Peachtree Summit
401 West Peachtree Street, NE
Atlanta, GA 30308

J. Walter Thompson U.S.A., Inc.
Experienced in: bank, investment, insurance, image, and visit-our-office
   advertising
2828 Tower Place
3340 Peachtree Road, NE
Atlanta, GA 30026

ILLINOIS

Chicago

N W Ayer Incorporated
Experienced in: bank, investment, insurance, image, direct response, visit-our-
   office, and tombstone advertising
One Illinois Center
111 East Wacker Drive
Chicago, IL 60601

Bozell, Jacobs, Kenyon & Eckhardt, Inc.
Experienced in: bank, investment, insurance, image, direct response, and tomb-
   stone advertising
Case history in Chapter 10 (Citizens & Southern Bank of South Carolina)
625 North Michigan Avenue
Chicago, IL 60611

Leo Burnett Inc.
Experienced in: bank and insurance advertising
Founded: 1935

Prudential Plaza
130 East Randolph Street
Chicago, IL 60601

Cunningham & Walsh, Inc.

Experienced in: bank, insurance, image, and direct response advertising
444 North Michigan Avenue, Suite 1400
Chicago, IL 60611

D'Arcy Masius Benton & Bowles Inc.

Experienced in: bank, insurance, image, and direct response advertising
200 East Randolph Drive
Chicago, IL 60601

Doremus & Company

Experienced in: bank, investment, insurance, image, direct response, and tomb-
    stone advertising
Case history following Chapter 2 (Standard & Poor's)
500 North Michigan Avenue
Chicago, IL 60611

Fletcher/Mayo/Associates Inc.

Experienced in: bank, investment, insurance, image, direct response, and visit-
    our-office advertising
211 East Ontario, 15th Floor
Chicago, IL 60611

Foote, Cone & Belding Communications, Inc.

Experienced in: bank, investment, insurance, image, direct response, and visit-
    our-office advertising
Founded: 1873
401 North Michigan Avenue
Chicago, IL 60611

Grey Advertising Inc.

Experienced in: bank, investment, insurance, image, direct response, and visit-
    our-office advertising
Case history in and following Chapter 1 (Bank of America)
Merchandise Mart
Chicago, IL 60654

HBM/Creamer, Inc.

Experienced in: bank, insurance, image, and direct response advertising
410 North Michigan Avenue
Chicago, IL 60611

Ketchum Communications, Inc.

Experienced in: bank, investment, insurance, image, and direct response
    advertising
Case histories in Chapter 9 (Pittsburgh National Bank and Union Trust Bank)

405 North Wabash Avenue-Suite P–3
River Plaza
Chicago, IL 60611

Mandabach & Simms, Inc.
Experienced in: bank, investment, image, direct response, and visit-our-office
advertising
Founded: 1952
111 North Canal Street
Chicago, IL 60606

Needham Harper Worldwide, Inc.
Experienced in: bank, insurance, image, and visit-our-office advertising
303 East Wacker Drive
Chicago, IL 60601

Ogilvy & Mather Advertising
Experienced in: bank, investment, insurance, image, direct response, and tombstone advertising
Case histories following Chapter 3 (California First Bank) and Chapter 5 (Nationwide Insurance)
676 St. Clair
Chicago, IL 60611

Soskin/Thompson Associates
Experienced in: bank, investment, and insurance direct response advertising
The John Hancock Center
875 North Michigan Avenue
Chicago, IL 60611

Tatham-Laird & Kudner
Experienced in: bank, image, direct response, and visit-our-office advertising
Founded: 1946
625 North Michigan Avenue
Chicago, IL 60611

J. Walter Thompson U.S.A., Inc.
Experienced in: bank, investment, insurance, image, and visit-our-office
advertising
875 North Michigan Avenue
Chicago, IL 60611

Wells, Rich, Greene, Inc.
Experienced in: bank, image and visit-our-office advertising
111 East Wacker Drive
Chicago, IL 60601

Young & Rubicam, Inc.
Experienced in: bank, investment, image, and visit-our-office advertising
111 East Wacker Drive
Chicago, IL 60601

Oak Brook

Bozell, Jacobs, Kenyon & Eckhardt, Inc.
Experienced in: bank, investment, insurance, image, and visit-our-office advertising
Case history in Chapter 10 (Citizens & Southern Bank of South Carolina)
1121 West Twenty-second Street, Suite 830
Oak Brook, IL 60521

Rosemont

Doyle Dane Bernbach Group Inc.
Experienced in: bank, investment, insurance, image, and visit-our-office advertising
Case history in Chapter 1 (CIGNA)
9801 West Higgins, Suite 220
Rosemont, IL 60018

INDIANA

Indianapolis

J. Walter Thompson U.S.A., Inc.
Experienced in: bank, investment, insurance, image, and visit-our-office advertising
9292 North Meridian Street, Suite 201
Indianapolis, IN 46260

Zionsville

Fairfax Advertising, Inc.
Experienced in: investment, insurance, image, and direct response advertising
25 East Cedar Street
Zionsville, IN 46077

IOWA

Waterloo

Colle & McVoy Advertising Agency, Inc.
Experienced in: bank, investment, insurance, image, visit-our-office, and direct response advertising

3606 Kimball Avenue
Waterloo, IA 50702

KANSAS

Overland Park

J. Walter Thompson U.S.A., Inc.
Experienced in: bank, investment, insurance, image, and visit-our-office
   advertising
10983 Granada Lane, Suite 310
Overland Park, KS 66211

KENTUCKY

Louisville

McCann Erickson Inc.
Experienced in: bank, investment, insurance, image, and visit-our-office
   advertising
1469 South Fourth Street
P.O. Box 1137
Louisville, KY 40208

J. Walter Thompson U.S.A., Inc.
Experienced in: bank, investment, insurance, image, and visit-our-office
   advertising
Suite 750, STM Plaza East
10101 Linn Station Road
Louisville, KY 40223

LOUISIANA

Metairie

Bozell, Jacobs, Kenyon & Eckhardt, Inc.
Experienced in: bank, investment, insurance, image, and visit-our-office
   advertising
Case history in Chapter 10 (Citizens & Southern Bank of South Carolina)
6620 Riverside Drive, Suite 311
Metairie, LA 70003

New Orleans

J. Walter Thompson U.S.A., Inc.
Experienced in: bank, investment, insurance, image, and visit-our-office advertising
1001 Howard Avenue, Suite 2305
New Orleans, LA 70113

MAINE

Portland

Arnold & Company Incorporated
Experienced in: bank, investment, insurance, image, and direct response advertising
949 Brighton Avenue
Portland, ME 04102

MARYLAND

Baltimore

Earle Palmer Brown Companies (The)
Experienced in: bank, investment, insurance, image, and direct response advertising
100 St. Paul Plaza, Suite 500
Baltimore, MD 21202

Davis, Johnson, Mogul & Colombatto, Inc.
Experienced in: bank, investment, insurance, image, direct response, visit-our-office, and tombstone advertising
Founded: 1957
Two Hamill Road, Suite 141
The Quadrangle, Village of Cross Keys
Baltimore, MD 21210

W. B. Doner and Company
Experienced in: bank, image and direct response advertising
2305 North Charles Street
Baltimore, MD 21218

Bethesda

Earle Palmer Brown Companies (The)
Experienced in: bank, investment, insurance, image, and direct response advertising
Founded: 1952
6935 Arlington Road
Bethesda, MD 20814

Rockville

Ketchum Communications, Inc.
Experienced in: bank, investment, insurance, image, and direct response advertising
Case histories in Chapter 9 (Pittsburgh National Bank and Union Trust Bank)
One Central Plaza, 11400 Rockville Pike
Rockville, MD 20852

MASSACHUSETTS

Boston

Arnold & Company Inc.
Experienced in: bank, investment, insurance, image, and direct response advertising
Founded: 1946
Park Square Building
Boston, MA 02116

Bozell, Jacobs, Kenyon & Eckhardt, Inc.
Experienced in: bank, investment, insurance, image, and visit-our-office advertising
Case history in Chapter 10 (Citizens & Southern Bank of South Carolina)
One Boston Place
Boston, MA 02108

Harold Cabot & Co., Inc.
Experienced in: bank, investment, insurance, image, direct response, and visit-our-office advertising
Case history in Chapter 8 (Fidelity USA)
Founded: 1930
One Constitution Plaza
Boston, MA 02129

Doremus & Company
Experienced in: bank, investment, insurance, image, direct response, and tombstone advertising
Case history following Chapter 2 (Standard & Poor's)
535 Boylston Street
Boston, MA 02116

HBM/Creamer, Inc.
Experienced in: bank, insurance, image, and direct response advertising
One Beacon Street
Boston, MA 02108

Hill, Holliday, Connors, Cosmopulos, Inc.
Experienced in: bank, investment, insurance, image, and direct response advertising
Founded: 1968
200 Clarendon Street, Hancock Tower
Boston, MA 02116

Ingalls Associates, Inc.
Experienced in: bank, investment, insurance, image, direct response, and visit-our-office advertising
Founded: 1911
2 Copley Place
Boston, MA 02116

Braintree

Bozell, Jacobs, Kenyon & Eckhardt, Inc.
Experienced in: bank, investment, insurance, image, and visit-our-office advertising
Case history in Chapter 10 (Citizens & Southern Bank of South Carolina)
75 Hancock Street
Braintree, MA 02184

MICHIGAN

Birmingham

Bozell, Jacobs, Kenyon & Eckhardt, Inc.
Experienced in: bank, investment, insurance, image, and visit-our-office advertising
Case history in Chapter 10 (Citizens & Southern Bank of South Carolina)
30600 Telegraph Road
Birmingham, MI 48010

Bloomfield Hills

D'Arcy Masius Benton & Bowles Inc.
Experienced in: bank, insurance, image, and direct response advertising
1725 North Woodward Avenue
P.O. Box 811
Bloomfield Hills, MI 48303

Detroit

N W Ayer Incorporated
Experienced in: bank, investment, insurance, image, direct response, visit-our-office, and tombstone advertising
2000 Fisher Building
Detroit, MI 48202

Ross Roy Inc.
Experienced in: insurance and image advertising
2751 East Jefferson Avenue
Detroit, MI 48207

J. Walter Thompson U.S.A., Inc.
Experienced in: bank, investment, insurance, image, and visit-our-office advertising
600 Renaissance Center
Detroit, MI 48243

Wells, Rich, Greene, Inc.
Experienced in: bank, image, and visit-our-office advertising
400 Renaissance Center Drive, Suite 808
Detroit, MI 48243

Wunderman, Ricotta & Kline Incorporated
Experienced in: bank, investment, insurance, image, direct response, visit-our-office, and tombstone advertising
200 Renaissance Tower
Detroit, MI 48243

Young & Rubicam Inc.
Experienced in: bank, investment, insurance, image, and direct response advertising
200 Renaissance Tower, Suite 1000
Detroit, MI 48243–1283

Southfield

Batten, Barton, Durstine & Osborn, Inc.
Experienced in: bank, investment, image, and visit-our-office advertising
26261 Evergreen Road
Southfield, MI 48086

W. B. Doner & Company
Experienced in: bank, image, and direct response advertising
Founded: 1937
26711 Northwestern Highway
Southfield, MI 48034

Saatchi & Saatchi Compton Inc.
Experienced in: investment, insurance, image, and direct response advertising
American Center Building
27777 Franklin Road
Southfield, MI 48034

Troy

Doyle Dane Bernbach Group Inc.
Experienced in: bank, investment, insurance, image, and visit-our-office
advertising
Case history in Chapter 1 (CIGNA)
Top of Troy Building
755 West Big Beaver Road
Troy, MI 48084

McCann Ericson Inc.
Experienced in: bank, investment, insurance, image, and visit-our-office
advertising
755 West Big Beaver Road
Troy, MI 48084

MINNESOTA

Bloomington

D'Arcy Masius Benton & Bowles Inc.
Experienced in: bank, insurance, image, and direct response advertising
7900 Xerxes Avenue South, Suite 600
Bloomington, MN 55431

Minneapolis

Batten, Barton, Durstine & Osborn, Inc.
Experienced in: bank, investment, image, and visit-our-office advertising
900 Brotherhood Building
625 Fourth Avenue South
Minneapolis, MN 55415

Bozell, Jacobs, Kenyon & Eckhardt, Inc.
Experienced in: bank, investment, insurance, image, direct response, and tombstone advertising
Case history in Chapter 10 (Citizens & Southern Bank of South Carolina)
Butler Square
100 North Sixth Street
Minneapolis, MN 55403

Campbell-Mithun, Inc.
Experienced in: bank, investment, and insurance image advertising
Founded: 1933
222 South Ninth Street
Minneapolis, MN 55402

Colle & McVoy Advertising Agency, Inc.
Experienced in: bank, investment, insurance, image, visit-our-office, and direct response advertising
Founded: 1935
700 International Plaza
Minneapolis, MN 55420

Grey Advertising Inc.
Experienced in: bank, investment, insurance, image, direct response, and visit-our-office advertising
Case history in and following Chapter 1 (Bank of America)
1000 Midwest Plaza East
Minneapolis, MN 55402

MISSOURI

Kansas City

Bozell, Jacobs, Kenyon & Eckhardt, Inc.
Experienced in: bank, investment, insurance, image, direct response, and tombstone advertising
Case history in Chapter 10 (Citizens & Southern Bank of South Carolina)
9233 Ward Parkway—Suite 124
Kansas City, MO 64114

Fletcher/Mayo/Associates, Inc.
Experienced in: bank, investment, insurance, image, direct response, and visit-our-office advertising
427 West Twelfth Street
Kansas City, MO 64105

St. Ann

Bozell, Jacobs, Kenyon & Eckhardt, Inc.
Experienced in: bank, investment, insurance, image, and visit-our-office advertising
Case history in Chapter 10 (Citizens & Southern Bank of South Carolina)
500 Northwest Plaza, Suite 911A
St. Ann, MO 63074

J. Walter Thompson U.S.A., Inc.
Experienced in: bank, investment, insurance, image, and visit-our-office advertising
500 Northwest Plaza, Suite 809
St. Ann, MO 63704

St. Joseph

Fletcher/Mayo/Associates Inc.
Experienced in: bank, investment, insurance, image, direct response, and visit-our-office advertising
Founded: 1957
Post Office Box B
John Glenn Road
St. Joseph, MO 64505

St. Louis

D'Arcy Masius Benton & Bowles Inc.
Experienced in: bank, insurance, image, and direct response advertising
1 Memorial Drive
St. Louis, MO 63102

Springfield

M A P Advertising Agency, Inc.
Experienced in: bank, investment, insurance, and image advertising
Founded: 1969
212 West McDaniel, P.O. Box 1836
Springfield, MO 65806

NEBRASKA

Omaha

Bozell, Jacobs, Kenyon & Eckhardt, Inc.
Experienced in: bank, investment, insurance, image, direct response advertising
Case history in Chapter 10 (Citizens & Southern Bank of South Carolina)
10250 Regency Circle
Omaha, NE 68114

J. Walter Thompson U.S.A., Inc.
Experienced in: bank, investment, insurance, image, and visit-our-office
   advertising
11128 John Galt Boulevard, Suite 552
Omaha, NE 68137

NEW JERSEY

Montclair

David H. Block Advertising
Experienced in: bank, investment, insurance, image, direct response, visit-our-
   office, and tombstone advertising
Founded: 1931
33 South Fullerton Avenue
Montclair, NJ 07042

Union

Bozell, Jacobs, Kenyon & Eckhardt, Inc.
Experienced in: bank, investment, insurance, image, direct response, and tomb-
   stone advertising
Case history in Chapter 10 (Citizens & Southern Bank of South Carolina)
2700 Route 22
Union, NJ 07083

NEW YORK

Albany

Arnold & Company Incorporated
Experienced in: bank, investment, insurance, image, and direct response
   advertising
Two Computer Drive West
Albany, NY 12205

Fairport

J. Walter Thompson U.S.A., Inc.
Experienced in: bank, investment, insurance, image, and visit-our-office
  advertising
Bushnells Basin
2815 Baird Road
Fairport, NY 14450

Rochester

Arnold & Company Incorporated
Experienced in: bank, investment, insurance, image, and direct response
  advertising
100 White Spruce Boulevard, Southview Commons
Rochester, NY 14623

Rumrill-Hoyt, Inc.
Experienced in: bank, image, direct response, and tombstone advertising
1895 Mount Hope Avenue, P.O. Box 1011
Rochester, NY 14603

Syracuse

Arnold & Company Incorporated
Experienced in: bank, investment, insurance, image, and direct response
  advertising
731 James Street
Syracuse, NY 13202

Bozell, Jacobs, Kenyon & Eckhardt, Inc.
Experienced in: bank, investment, insurance, image, and visit-our-office
  advertising
Case history in Chapter 10 (Citizens & Southern Bank of South Carolina)
201 South Main Street, Suite 7
North Syracuse, NY 13212

NORTH CAROLINA

Charlotte

J. Walter Thompson U.S.A., Inc.
Experienced in: bank, investment, insurance, image, and visit-our-office
  advertising
4801 Independence Boulevard, Suite 708
Charlotte, NC 28212

Raleigh

McKinney Silver & Rockett, Inc.
Experienced in: bank, investment, image, direct response, visit-our-office, and
tombstone advertising
Founded: 1969
333 Fayetteville Street
Raleigh, NC 27601

OHIO

Cincinnati

Bozell, Jacobs, Kenyon & Eckhardt, Inc.
Experienced in: bank, investment, insurance, image, and visit-our-office
advertising
Case history in Chapter 10 (Citizens & Southern Bank of South Carolina)
8160 Corporate Park Drive, Suite 106
Cincinnati, OH 45242

Cleveland

Marschalk Company, Inc. (The)
Experienced in: bank, investment, and insurance image advertising
601 Rockwell Avenue
Cleveland, OH 44114

Wyse Advertising, Inc.
Experienced in: bank image advertising
Founded: 1951
24 Public Square
Cleveland, OH 44113

Dayton

Yeck Brothers Group
Experienced in: bank, investment, insurance, image, direct response, and visit-
our-office advertising
Case history in Chapter 2 (AmeriTrust Corporation)
Founded: 1946
2222 Arbor Boulevard
Dayton, OH 45439

Mansfield

Mandabach & Simms, Inc.
Experienced in: bank, investment, image, direct response, and visit-our-office
advertising
1277 Lexington Avenue
Mansfield, OH 44907

OKLAHOMA

Oklahoma City

J. Walter Thompson U.S.A., Inc.
Experienced in: bank, investment, insurance, image, and visit-our-office
advertising
50 Penn Place, Suite 1208
Oklahoma City, OK 73118

OREGON

Beaverton

Batten, Barton, Durstine & Osborn, Inc.
Experienced in: bank, investment, image, and visit-our-office advertising
10550 Southwest Allen Avenue, Suite 101
Beaverton, OR 97005

Bozell, Jacobs, Kenyon & Eckhardt, Inc.
Experienced in: bank, investment, insurance, image, and visit-our-office
advertising
Case history in Chapter 10 (Citizens & Southern Bank of South Carolina)
12655 SW Center, Suite 565
Beaverton, OR 97005

Portland

Davis, Johnson, Mogul & Colombatto, Inc.
Experienced in: bank, investment, insurance, image, direct response, visit-our-
office, and tombstone advertising
1001 Southwest Fifth Avenue, Suite 1000
Portland, OR 97204

Evans Communications, Inc.
Experienced in: bank, investment, insurance, image, direct response, visit-our-office, and tombstone advertising
620 Morgan Building
Portland, OR 97205

PENNSYLVANIA

Bala Cynwyd

J. Walter Thompson U.S.A., Inc.
Experienced in: bank, investment, insurance, image, and visit-our-office advertising
555 East City Line Avenue
Bala Cynwyd, PA 19004

Philadelphia

Kalish & Rice Inc.
Experienced in: bank, investment, insurance, image, and direct response advertising
1845 Walnut Street
Philadelphia, PA 19103

Ketchum Communications, Inc.
Experienced in: bank, investment, insurance, image, and direct response advertising
Case histories in Chapter 9 (Pittsburgh National Bank and Union Trust Bank)
615 Chestnut Street
Philadelphia, PA 19106

Al Paul Lefton Co. Inc.
Experienced in: insurance, direct response, and visit-our-office advertising
Founded: 1928
Rohm & Haas Building
Independence Mall West
Philadelphia, PA 19106

Lewis, Gilman & Kynett Inc.
Experienced in: bank image and direct response advertising
Founded: 1983
1700 Market Street
Philadelphia, PA 19103

Narcisso-Volz
Experienced in: bank and image advertising
Founded: 1974
1900 Packard Building
111 South Fifteenth Street
Philadelphia, PA 19102

Reimel Carter Advertising, Inc.
Experienced in: bank, investment, insurance, image, direct response, visit-our-office, and tombstone advertising
Founded: 1962
1420 Locust Street
Philadelphia, PA 19102

Spiro & Associates Incorporated
Experienced in: bank, investment, insurance, image, direct response, visit-our-office, and tombstone advertising
Founded: 1933
100 South Broad Street
Philadelphia, PA 19110

Pittsburgh

Bozell, Jacobs, Kenyon & Eckhardt, Inc.
Experienced in: bank, investment, insurance, image, and visit-our-office advertising
Case history in Chapter 10 (Citizens & Southern Bank of South Carolina)
1910 Cochran Road, Manor Oaks Two, Suite 639
Pittsburgh, PA 15219

Brouillard Communications
Experienced in: bank, investment, insurance, image, and direct response advertising
Case history in Chapter 5 (Irving Trust)
600 Grant Street
Pittsburgh, PA 15219

HBM/Creamer, Inc.
Experienced in: bank, insurance, image, and direct response advertising
600 Grant Street
Pittsburgh, PA 15219

Ketchum Communications, Inc.
Experienced in: bank, investment, insurance, image, and direct response advertising
Founded: 1923
Case histories in Chapter 9 (Pittsburgh National Bank and Union Trust Bank)

Six PPG Place
Pittsburgh, PA 15222

RHODE ISLAND

Providence

HBM/Creamer, Inc.
Experienced in: bank, insurance, image, and direct response advertising
800 Turks Head Building
Providence, RI 02903

TENNESSEE

Memphis

Bozell, Jacobs, Kenyon & Eckhardt, Inc.
Experienced in: bank, investment, insurance, image, and visit-our-office
    advertising
Case history in Chapter 10 (Citizens & Southern Bank of South Carolina)
% Chrysler Corporation
P.O. Box 18050
Memphis, TN 38118

J. Walter Thompson U.S.A., Inc.
Experienced in: bank, investment, insurance, image, and visit-our-office
    advertising
White Station Tower Building, Suite 1715
5050 Poplar Street
Memphis, TN 38157

TEXAS

Dallas

Bozell, Jacobs, Kenyon & Eckhardt, Inc.
Experienced in: bank, investment, insurance, image, direct response advertising
Case history in Chapter 10 (Citizens & Southern Bank of South Carolina)
201 East Carpenter Freeway
Dallas/Fort Worth Airport
Dallas, TX 75261–9200

McCann Erickson Inc.
Experienced in: bank, investment, insurance, image, and visit-our-office
    advertising
10830 North Central Expressway, Suite 246
Dallas, TX 75231

Ogilvy & Mather Advertising
Experienced in: bank, investment, insurance, image, direct response, and tomb-
    stone advertising
Case histories following Chapter 3 (California First Bank) and Chapter 5 (Na-
    tionwide Insurance)
14840 Landmark Boulevard, Suite 290
Dallas, TX 75240

J. Walter Thompson U.S.A., Inc.
Experienced in: bank, investment, insurance, image, and visit-our-office
    advertising
12700 Park Central Drive, Suite 303
Dallas, TX 75251

Tracy-Locke Advertising, Inc.
Experienced in: bank, investment, insurance, image, direct response, visit-our-
    office, and tombstone advertising
Founded: 1913
600 North Pearl
Dallas, TX 75201

Houston

Bozell, Jacobs, Kenyon & Eckhardt, Inc.
Experienced in: bank, investment, insurance, image, direct response, and tomb-
    stone advertising
Case history in Chapter 10 (Citizens & Southern Bank of South Carolina)
Republic Bank Center, No. 3300
700 Louisiana Street
Houston, TX 77002

D'Arcy Masius Benton & Bowles, Inc.
Experienced in: bank, investment, insurance, image, and direct response
    advertising
Case history following Chapter 7 (E. F. Hutton & Company)
2000 West Loop South
Houston, TX 77027

W. B. Doner & Company
Experienced in: bank, image, and direct response advertising
2900 Wesleyan, Suite 650
Houston, TX 77027

Ketchum Communications, Inc.
Experienced in: bank, investment, insurance, image, and direct response
  advertising
Case histories in Chapter 9 (Pittsburgh National Bank and Union Trust Bank)
1900 West Loop South, Suite 1300
Houston, TX 77027

McCann Erickson Inc.
Experienced in: bank, investment, insurance, image, and visit-our-office
  advertising
520 Post Oak Boulevard
Houston, TX 77027

Marschalk Company, Inc. (The)
Experienced in: bank, investment, and insurance image advertising
7322 Southwest Freeway, Suite 1000
Houston, TX 77074

Ogilvy & Mather Advertising
Experienced in: bank, investment, insurance, image, direct response, and tombstone advertising
Case histories following Chapter 3 (California First Bank) and Chapter 5 (Nationwide Insurance)
1415 Louisiana Street
Houston, TX 77002

J. Walter Thompson U.S.A., Inc.
Experienced in: bank, investment, insurance, image, and visit-our-office
  advertising
West Chase National Bank Building
9801 Westheimer, Suite 606
Houston, TX 77042

UTAH

Murray

Francom Advertising, Inc.
Experienced in: bank advertising
Founded: 1939
5282 South 320 West, Suite D–100
Murray, UT 84107

Salt Lake City

Bozell, Jacobs, Kenyon & Eckhardt, Inc.
Experienced in: bank, investment, insurance, image, direct response, and tombstone advertising
Case history in Chapter 10 (Citizens & Southern Bank of South Carolina)
First Interstate Plaza
120 South Main Street, No. 1230
Salt Lake City, UT 84101

Evans Communications, Inc.
Experienced in: bank, investment, insurance, image, direct response, visit-our-office, and tombstone advertising
Founded: 1943
4 Triad Center, Suite 750
Salt Lake City, UT 84180

J. Walter Thompson U.S.A., Inc.
Experienced in: bank, investment, insurance, image, and visit-our-office advertising
John Hancock Center
455 South Third East
Salt Lake City, UT 84111

VIRGINIA

Alexandria

Bozell, Jacobs, Kenyon & Eckhardt, Inc.
Experienced in: bank, investment, insurance, image, direct response, and tombstone advertising
Case history in Chapter 10 (Citizens & Southern Bank of South Carolina)
1199 North Fairfax Street, Suite 804
Alexandria, VA 22314

McLean

Needham Harper Worldwide, Inc.
Experienced in: bank, investment, insurance, image, and direct response advertising
8300 Greensboro Drive
McLean, VA 22102

Richmond

Earle Palmer Brown Companies (The)
Experienced in: bank, investment, insurance, image, and direct response
advertising
7814 Carousel Lane, Suite 300
Richmond, VA 23229

J. Walter Thompson U.S.A., Inc.
Experienced in: bank, investment, insurance, image, and visit-our-office
advertising
Heritage Building, Suite 825
1001 East Main Street
Richmond, VA 23219

Roanoke

Houck & Harrison
Experienced in: bank, insurance, image, and direct response advertising
Case history following Chapter 2 (Blue Cross and Blue Shield of Southwestern
Virginia)
Founded: 1928
1402 Grandin Road SW, P.O. Box 12487
Roanoke, VA 24026

WASHINGTON

Seattle

Evans/Kraft, Inc.
Experienced in: bank, investment, insurance, image, direct response, visit-our-
office, and tombstone advertising
190 Queen Anne Avenue North
Seattle, WA 98109

McCann Erickson Inc.
Experienced in: bank, investment, insurance, image, and visit-our-office
advertising
1001 Fourth Avenue
Seattle, WA 98154

Allen Nelson & Co., Incorporated
Experienced in: bank, investment, direct response, and tombstone advertising
Founded: 1977
P.O. Box 16157
4517 Glenn Way, SW
Seattle, WA 98116

INDEX

About the Author

ALEC BENN, one of a handful of pioneers of modern financial advertising, is widely recognized as the foremost authority on the advertising of financial products and services. President and chief executive of the advertising firm of Benn & MacDonough, he is the author of *The 27 Most Common Mistakes in Advertising* and *The 23 Most Common Mistakes in Public Relations*.